COLLINS Family Pet Guides

KU-481-222

GUINEA PIG

Peter Gurney

First published in 1999 by
HarperCollins_Publishers_
77-85 Fulham Palace Road
Hammersmith
London W6 8JB

Collins is a registered trademark of
HarperCollins Publishers Limited

The HarperCollins website address
is www.**fire**and**water**.com

04 03 02 01 00 99

9 8 7 6 5 4 3 2 1

© HarperCollins*Publishers* Ltd 1999

Peter Gurney asserts the moral
right to be identified as the author
of this work.

A catalogue record of this book is
available from the British Library.

ISBN 0 00 413388 9

THIS BOOK WAS CREATED BY
SP Creative Design for
HarperCollins_Publishers_ **Ltd**
EDITOR: Heather Thomas
DESIGN AND PRODUCTION:
Rolando Ugolini
PHOTOGRAPHY: Bruce Tanner
ADDITIONAL PHOTOGRAPHY:
Peter Gurney and Rolando Ugolini

COLOUR REPRODUCTION BY
Saxon Photolitho Ltd, Norwich
PRINTED AND BOUND BY
Rotolito Lombarda SpA, Italy

Contents

Introduction

Guinea pigs are becoming increasingly popular both in the UK and many other countries as pets. However, it was not long after I had acquired my first guinea pig that I realized that there was very little accurate information about their husbandry and veterinary care. The past twelve years of my life have been dedicated to gathering such information and making it more widely available.

Guinea pigs are the ideal house pets, although many of these gentle creatures are still kept outdoors in hutches. However, modern thinking is that it is often better for both the animal and its human owner when they live together, and I hope that by the end of this book the reasons for this will be only too obvious to you.

Guinea pigs which are housed inside their owner's home are very laid back compared with the hutched kind of guinea pig. They soon become accustomed to the large noisy human animals with whom they share their home tottering around on their hind legs. They know that these humans are quite harmless, good at foraging for food for them, and that they respond well when squeaked at.

Guinea pigs have lots of advantages as house pets. They are practically odourless, are very cheap to feed and maintain, easy to handle and rarely bite. In a way, the last point can be a disadvantage from the animal's point of view and this is why it is always advisable for parents to supervise young children when they handle guinea pigs. If a child mishandles a cat or a dog it will let him/her know very quickly with its teeth or claws, or it will usually be strong and agile enough to wriggle out of the child's grasp. As a guinea pig is far less robust and is not likely to bite, the only sanction it has is to squeak its protest which is not sufficient to deter clumsy handling.

In Britain, the United States and many European countries, guinea pigs are kept as pets and as show animals and it is easy to understand their appeal. They are a cosy, cob-shaped handful for an adult and a comfortable armful for a child, and are usually very amenable to human handling.

The biggest misconception about guinea pigs is, and even many animal experts say this, that they are bovine and without personality. This only goes to prove that those who think this have never actually had the pleasure of living with guinea pigs.

However these animals are housed, indoors or outside, I hope that this book will encourage people to handle their guinea pigs more and to take on the responsibility of attending to their basic veterinary needs. The lives of the owners and their pets will be greatly enhanced if they do so.

CHAPTER ONE

Origins and history

How guinea pigs acquired their name is a bit of a puzzle and there is much debate about it. The animal does not come from Guinea and is not a pig, despite its scientific name of cavia porcellus, *(pig-like cavy). This endearing rodent is a native of South America and can still be found there in the mountains and grasslands of Peru, Argentina and Uruguay.*

There are many theories as to how the 'guinea' part of the name came into use. In Britain, the word 'guinea' was once a term for anything foreign but if this is the case why are there not guinea lions, leopards and lemurs?

When guinea pigs were first introduced to the British Isles in the sixteenth century they were very rare and perhaps a guinea (twenty-one shillings) was the usual price for one. Anything priced in guineas was usually considered valuable and guinea pigs would certainly have had a rarity value.

They were brought to Europe a little earlier in the sixteenth century from Dutch Guiana so could guinea pig be a corruption of 'Guiana'? Perhaps, but Europe is the one place where the word 'guinea' has no connection with the animal. The term used in most European countries translates into 'sea pig' and in Russia they are called *Moskaya svinka* which means sea pig. This name is derived from the fact that sailors brought them back to Europe.

Italy has a particularly charming name for guinea pigs and this brings us to the last theory of the guinea derivation. The Italian name is *porcellino da India* (little pig of India). Did these animals arrive in Italy and England from the Dutch East Indies, which includes New Guinea, in ships that had crossed the Pacific from South America to pick up cargoes in the East Indies? Both the English and the Dutch were trading or expanding their interests in South America at around this time. As the Dutch, English and Italians were all engaged in the spice trade, which was then firmly established in the East Indies, perhaps the 'guinea' is really derived from New Guinea.

It does not take much deep thought to deduce how the 'pig' part of the name came to be used. Guinea pigs are short necked with long bodies which are carried low to the ground upon short legs. They squeak a lot and root around, constantly munching on this and that — rather like pigs, in fact.

In more 'serious' circles guinea pigs are usually referred to as 'Cavies'. This name is shorthand for the Latin word *caviidea* which was used to describe animals with short, or no, tails.

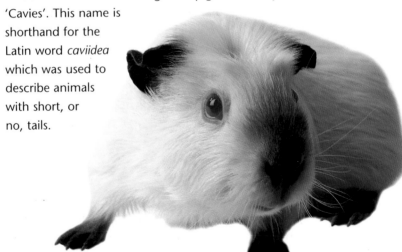

Above: *The guinea pig is a cautious, alert animal, constantly looking out for predators.*

Habitat equals anatomy

The wild guinea pig is a little smaller than the domesticated one and is very much more alert and ready to flee for its life. This is because it has to work harder for its living and flight is its best form of defence, so Mother Nature has decided, by the process of natural selection, that this leaner model has a better chance of survival in the wild.

Did you know?

One of the guinea pig's close relations is the porcupine. Another is the chinchilla; both are residents of South America.

In South America, where the guinea pig has long been a culinary delicacy, domestic guinea pigs are likely to be kept for food. By a process of fattening them up with kitchen scraps of vegetables and wheat products and breeding for the pot, guinea pigs have become larger animals. One of Pizarro's men, during the conquest of Peru, wrote: 'The Indians of Peru raise large quantities of small white animals, or of various colours, resembling, on a smaller scale, the rabbit which they call "Cuijes". They eat or sacrifice them to their gods.'

Although they are not eaten in most of the other countries in which they are now resident, guinea pigs have been kept as pets for a long time, and this, together with the growing interest in showing them, has resulted in larger guinea pigs all round, for most people prefer them to be chunky.

Digestive system and teeth

The guinea pig's natural habitat is the grasslands and plains that supply the herbivorous diet it requires. Guinea pigs are among a minority of animals (including human beings) that must obtain their vitamin C by eating vegetable matter. Grass is not only rich in vitamin C but it is also very fibrous, which is another vital requirement for the guinea pig's digestive system. They also need most of the B vitamins and minerals that we require and in the wild they obtain these mainly from the seeds and grains of grasses.

The warm, dry climate of South America does not produce the same kind of lush, succulent grass as does our damp and often cold one, and thus the guinea pig spends a great deal of its

Above: *Domestic guinea pigs, like their wild cousins, love eating fresh grass.*

Right: *The incisor teeth are powerful but are seldom used in anger.*

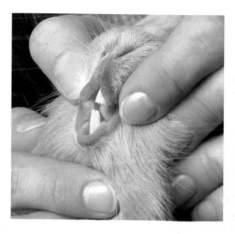

time grazing so as to get sufficient nutrition from the drier, brittle grasses of the plains. Fortunately, it is very well equipped for this task. It has upper and lower incisor teeth positioned centrally at the front of the jaws, while behind them, deep in the mouth, are the premolars and molars which are very similar to our own teeth but more V-shaped with the apex of the 'V' pointing out towards the mouth. The big difference between our teeth and those of the guinea pig is that the guinea pig's are rootless and continuously growing. This is essential for keeping up with the heavy work load with which they have to contend and grinding down the high-fibre diet they need to stay fit and healthy. If guinea pigs had our kind of teeth, they would quickly be ground down to gum level!

It is important to be aware of the dentition of guinea pigs because their teeth are vital for the maintenance of general good health. Many people call them eating machines, and as they munch away for most of the time when they are not dozing, it is indeed a good description of them.

Did you know?

There has been some debate in distinguished zoological circles in recent years as to whether the guinea pig has been misclassified and whether it is really a rodent.

Above: *Guinea pigs are very inquisitive creatures and enjoy investigating new environments.*

The senses

■ **Sight:** The eyesight of a guinea pig cannot match ours in the perception of detail, but it is extremely adept at picking up quick movements, particularly from above. Birds of prey are among their natural predators in the wild so this makes sense from an evolutionary point of view, as does the fact that their eyes are set high in the head.

■ **Smell:** The sense of smell varies enormously between animals, with some guinea pigs able to pick up the scent of even a small handful of grass being brought into a room whereas other

cannot even seem to scent parsley, one of their favourite treats, when it is placed under their noses.

■ **Hearing:** The one sense that is the most finely honed is that of hearing. It begins a little lower than our own range and extends way above it.

▌Body and coat

The guinea pig has very short legs in ratio to its long rotund body which is carried close to the ground, giving the animal a low centre of gravity. This makes it very stable when running and surprisingly agile.

Truly, these are animals with coats of many colours which can be subdivided into rough-, smooth- and long-haired varieties, and many of the various breeds take their names from either the texture, patterning or colour of these coats. Some of the most well-known breeds are listed on the following pages.

Did you know?

Many people worry that their guinea pigs are either over- or under-weight. Provided that the weight of the animal is proportional to its overall size, as is usually the case, then there should not be any problems. Just take a look at the human species which has a bewildering array of shapes and sizes!

CHAPTER ONE

BREEDS OF GUINEA PIG

Short-haired breeds

Rex

❖ *Rex*

■ *Appearance:* These short-coated guinea pigs are called teddies in America — a highly appropriate name as they do look like teddy bears. The coat is crinkled and frizzy and has a springy texture when touched.

Satin

■ *Appearance:* This variety has a wonderful satin sheen to its coat. An increasing number of satins are being cross-bred with long-haired varieties to enhance the effect even more. Close examination of the hair shafts show them to be slightly transparent which reflects the light off the coat, thereby imparting its distinctive sheen.

❖ *Satin*

Standard Self

■ *Appearance:* This is one of the most common breeds of all for it is simply a guinea pig with the same coloured short hair all over its body. The recognised colours for show quality Selfs are, black, white, cream, golden, red, chocolate, beige and lilac.

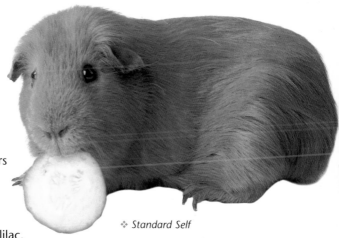

❖ *Standard Self*

▌Rough-coated breeds

Abyssinian

■ *Appearance:* This is a rough-coated variety with distinct whirls of hair in the coat. These are called rosettes and they have to be in particular positions, be of good depth and radiate from pinpoint centres to be of show quality. The neck rosettes push the hair forwards, giving the guinea pig a pair of glorious Victorian 'pork chop' whiskers. Viewed from the front, they always seem to have an expression of surprise.

❖ *Abyssinian*

▌Smooth-coated breeds

Agouti
■ *Appearance:* This is the kind of coat that is more common in the wild and resembles that of the common wild rabbit. The tips of the hairs are lighter than the shafts, creating a kind of shine on the coat.

❖ *Agouti*

Crested
■ *Appearance:* There are two basic types of crested guinea pig: the English and the American. Both sport a jaunty crest of hair which is shaped like one of the rosettes of an Abyssinian on top of the head. The English crest is the same colour as the rest of the coat but in the American the inside of the crest is pure white.

❖ *Lilac crested*

❖ *Dutch*

Dutch

▪ *Appearance:* The Dutch has a smooth coat with similar markings to the Friesian cow. There are panda-like patterns over the eyes, shoulders and rump on a white background.

▪ *Notes:* These guinea pigs must adhere to strict parameters if they are to be regarded as show quality.

Himalayan (standard and crested)

▪ *Appearance:* Anyone who has seen a Siamese cat would probably call one of these guinea pigs a Siamese breed. It has a similar pattern on its ears, snout and feet. It is called pointing and can be either chocolate or black. One line of this breed has the same kind of crest as the crested guinea pig whereas the standard has a smooth head.

❖ *Himalayan*

CHAPTER
ONE

Long-coated breeds

Coronet

■ *Appearance:* The Coronet has long, luscious locks which sweep down to the ground and which are parted up the middle of the spine. The name Coronet is derived from the one they wear upon their heads. It is similar to the Crested but far more elegant, with its rim fountaining down over the shoulders.

❖ *Coronets*

❖ *Peruvian*

Peruvian

▓ *Appearance:* Again, there is a neat comparison with another animal — this time, a dog. Peruvians wear the same kind of coat as a Skye terrier with a dash of Old English sheepdog thrown in. Their coats are long, parted down the spine and flow over the head, leaving them to peer out from behind a curtain of hair.

Sheltie

▓ *Appearance:* The Sheltie is identical to the Peruvian apart from the fact that it has a swept-back hairstyle on the head.

❖ *Sheltie*

CHAPTER
ONE

❖ *Argenti*

▎ Rare breeds

The guinea pigs featured on the previous pages are the most common breeds but there are also a few rare breeds including the following:

- Alpaca
- Argenti
- Bicolour
- Brindle

- Dalmatian
- Harlequin
- Magpie
- Merino

- Roan
- Texel
- Tortoiseshell

❖ *Texel*

The mongrel

The mongrel guinea pig is probably natural selection at its finest for, as a general rule of thumb, these animals live longer and have a tendency to be healthier than their pedigree companions. What it means in simple terms is that there is a very good mix of the gene pool. Mother Nature long ago determined that it was not good for any species to in-breed and this is why in all pack animals the males are usually hounded out of the pack as soon as they become fertile. The guinea pig shown above is a Crested mix.

CHAPTER TWO

Acquiring a guinea pig

Although guinea pigs must be among the most self maintaining of all pets, there are three essential tasks that they cannot carry out for themselves and that their owners must be prepared to do for them. They are as follows:

- *Shopping or foraging for food.*
- *Housework — mucking out their quarters on a regular basis.*
- *Being responsible for their veterinary care.*

Needless to say, by paying particular attention to the first two of these three chores, the last one will be made far easier. A clean and properly fed guinea pig is, by definition, a healthier one and this should help to prevent many common health problems occurring.

In the last chapter of this book, you will find comprehensive, up-to-date veterinary information which is aimed specifically at helping owners to diagnose and treat their own animals. However, if you are in any doubt at all, it is always advisable to consult your vet immediately rather than going it alone. There are times when professional veterinary care is required, but as this is not usually cheap, the more that owners can do to prevent health problems arising and to treat their own animals themselves, the better. Bear all these factors in mind before you decide to acquire a guinea pig.

Which sex?

Female guinea pigs are called sows, whereas males are known as boars, and the arrangement of their reproductive organs differs somewhat. This brings us to the first problem that a first-time owner is likely to encounter when trying to acquire a guinea pig.

I have given up counting the number of times that someone has rung me asking if I could home some baby guinea pigs that were 'unexpected'. Invariably it is because a sow has been sold to the owner when it was already pregnant, or two sows, or boars, have turned out to be one of each kind and the inevitable has occurred! Invariably, these animals have been acquired from a pet shop and although, of course, there are some wonderful pet shops around, there are far too few of them.

The best advice is to buy your pet(s) from a recommended breeder or from a more experienced keeper of guinea pigs. Alternatively, you could give a good home to some guinea pigs that have been taken in by animal charities.

Below: *A baby guinea pig discovering the feed bowl.*

Sexing a guinea pig

The two photographs below should act as a useful guide when your are sexing guinea pigs. The left one shows the sow whereas the right is the boar. Note the distinct raised dot in the two prongs of the 'Y' arrangement of the boar. It is because the boar's penis is completely retractable that mistakes can be made, but the raised ring is quite clear by the time the boar is about six weeks of age, when these photos were taken.

Above: *Although the penis is retracted, it is still very clear.*

Above: *The typical 'Y' configuration of the female genitalia.*

How many?

The only number that you should not consider is one! Guinea pigs are pack animals and enjoy the company of their own kind. In the case of sows, the number can be as many as you have room for. When it comes to the boars, then it is best to stick to two. Even experienced owners can seldom manage to get more than two boars to live harmoniously together.

CHAPTER TWO

Two boars will settle down quite contentedly as a pair if they are brothers, or even ones from different litters if they are introduced to one another after they have been weaned. Alternatively, an adult boar will accept a youngster of six to eight weeks of age.

However, a note of warning before you make up your mind. It is simply that you leave room for expansion, for very few people are strong willed enough to resist the temptation to have yet more guinea pigs. If you do decide right from the start to keep more than a couple, then it is best to stick to sows for they will live in large groups and one large pen or hutch is much easier to maintain than three or four, which would be necessary for housing pairs of boars.

Below: *Female guinea pigs (sows) will live very happily together.*

Did you know?

When you first put a young boar in with an adult, three house bricks are very useful. Place two of them side by side with a large enough gap for the baby guinea pig to get into, then place the other brick on top. Alternatively, use a piece of thick cardboard tube or a ceramic drain pipe which has a baby guinea pig-sized diameter. As the baby is usually impregnated with the scent of its mother, or simply because most boars are 'ambidextrous' sexually, a boar will usually try to mate with the baby! The brick arrangement or tube makes a very convenient bolt hole for the baby.

CHAPTER
TWO

▌Introducing other pets

If you already have a cat or a dog you will have to take time to gradually introduce them to the new 'animals on the block', so to speak. Remember that they think of your home as their territory so they have to get used to the newcomers. Make even more fuss of your dog or cat than usual and get them to sniff the guinea pigs while you have them on your lap. If they are to be kept indoors in open pens, then never leave them alone with

▌**Above:** *Introducing a guinea pig to a dog, especially a puppy, must be supervised by an adult. It is advisable to keep the dog on a very short lead in case he unexpectantly escapes from your grip.*

your cat or dog unless those pens can be
properly secured. Even the most amiable
dog or cat can have its wild instincts
aroused by the sight of a furry
little creature scurrying about.

Many guinea pig owners
find that their cats or dogs
become very affectionate and
even protective towards their
guinea pigs, especially if they are
housed indoors with them.

Choosing a guinea pig

The general view is that when choosing a puppy it is usually wise
to go for the one that comes bounding up to you and wants
to be petted. With baby guinea pigs, it is quite the reverse. The
healthy young guinea pig immediately races away from you
and finds somewhere to hide. This betokens an animal whose
nervous system is in fine fettle, and from the way that it runs you
can see that its limbs and lungs are in top form.

Above: *All guinea pigs look cute and cuddly but it is important
to choose a healthy animal.*

Health checks

There are a few quick
health checks that you
can make and it is always
best to carry these out
while you are sitting
down with the animal on
your lap.

1 & 2 Have a quick
check through the guinea
pig's coat by running the
tip of your finger against
the lay of the hair to see
if there are any scurfy or
bald spots which may be
indicative of a fungal or
parasitic skin condition.

3 Check that the teeth are not broken, that they impinge
evenly and that they are not loose. You must ensure also that
the nose is dry, the eyes are bright and that the guinea pig's
movements are urgent and vigorous.

Breeders and animal charities

If you are acquiring your guinea pigs from a reputable breeder who cares for his or her stock, then you won't be offered unhealthy animals. The breeder will certainly be pleased to know that the animal is going to someone who has taken the trouble to check up on the practical aspects of owning guinea pigs.

Those new to guinea pig keeping are sometimes reluctant to acquire their stock from animal charities on the grounds that the animals on offer are likely to be older. However, do not be put off by middle-aged guinea pigs. Although the pleasures of watching an animal grow into adulthood may have to be foregone, the rewards of giving a home to one of these refugees are endless. Many have been abandoned, ill treated or neglected and the pleasure comes in lavishing lots of tender loving care upon them that other humans have not.

I have taken many in and have known of other owners who have done so and it is generally agreed that once these animals have become accustomed to trusting the new human being in their lives, the response is wonderful. It usually takes time but gradually the timid, nervous creature you took under your wing becomes, firstly, more inquisitive about you and then bolder until in the end it trusts you and comes to you when called. To have an animal's trust is something very special indeed, especially when it has had to be worked for in the case of animals that have learned from experience to be wary of the human species!

CHAPTER THREE

Housing your guinea pig

I prefer to live with my guinea pigs so I keep mine indoors. However, guinea pigs can be kept outside provided that they are protected from extremes of weather and from other animals. This chapter focuses on what you need to provide for both indoor and outdoor accommodation.

The important thing to remember when it comes to housing guinea pigs is their country of origin; South America has a warm, dry climate. Yes, of course the weather can be hot, cold or wet outside there but the wild guinea pig's instincts are far more finely tuned than those of its domestic cousins. It can detect these climatic changes to some degree before they occur and can take avoiding action, seeking shelter from these extremes.

Traditional hutches

The captive domestic guinea pig in outdoor accommodation does not have the option of seeking out more comfortable spots when the weather changes so the owner must take this into account. By making accommodation mobile, especially if it is the traditional hutch type, you can save yourself a lot of expense and inconvenience. Flexibility and mobility are important.

Guinea pigs can be moved into a shed or conservatory during the winter or into more shaded areas in the heat of the summer. However, it is pleasing to note that during the past few years the manufacturers of all kinds of pet animal accommodation have been getting far more imaginative. What they are designing is not only more animal friendly, but it is also more aesthetically pleasing. In the case of guinea pig housing, they have designed some wonderful raked-roofed hutches, resembling children's Wendy houses, which are either split level or have as many as three or four floors in them. They usually have traps or sliding door arrangements which can shut off the guinea pigs in the upper floor, out of reach of predators, when the owners are away for any length of time.

Siting the hutch outside

Hutches should be secured 90–120 cm/36–48 in high against a wall or a sturdy fence. They can still be reasonably mobile if they are secured by pegs or catches. Although even the most arthritic cat could get onto all of these hutches, it usually loses interest in

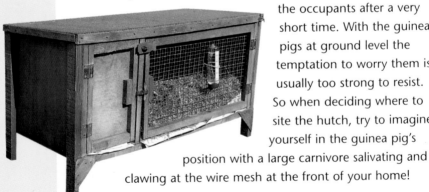

the occupants after a very short time. With the guinea pigs at ground level the temptation to worry them is usually too strong to resist. So when deciding where to site the hutch, try to imagine yourself in the guinea pig's position with a large carnivore salivating and clawing at the wire mesh at the front of your home!

Above: *All outdoor hutches should be raised off the ground and have a felt roof covering to protect the cage and the guinea pig from damp and rain.*

The ideal siting of outdoor accommodation is:
■ Out of the sun.
■ Shaded from the wind.
■ Not in a damp part of the garden.

One final point about outdoor accommodation: if chemical pest control sprays are used in the garden, avoid their use in the vicinity of your guinea pigs. If you live in the country and are close to agricultural land, find out if and when crop spraying is likely to take place and bring your animals indoors when it occurs. Wind drift from some of these sprays can be fatal to guinea pigs.

Also, in cold weather, cover the hutch at night with a blanket to keep the guinea pig(s) warm. You could even move the hutch into a garden shed or sheltered place.

Do-it-yourself

You do not have to buy a ready-made hutch, many of which are quite expensive. If you are good at carpentry, you could have a go at making one yourself. Indoor accommodation need only consist of a wooden box with a glass front. However, if making an outdoor hutch, you must weatherproof it.

Below: *Always choose a hutch that is raised off the ground (left).*

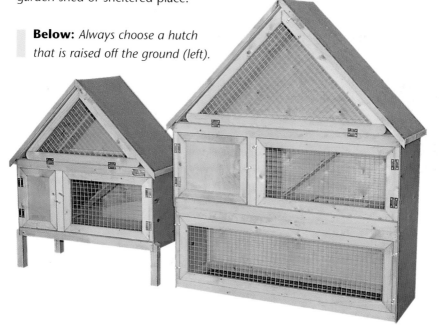

CHAPTER
THREE

Siting the hutch inside

Indoor accommodation is much less of a problem because considerations of climate do not come into the equation. Guinea pigs are comfortable in the same temperature ranges and types of humidity that we humans like to live in in our own homes. If there is a resident cat or dog, it can be kept either out of the room in which the guinea pigs live when the owner is not around or covers can be made for the tops of the pens. I do stress 'pens' for these are all that are needed.

This type of accommodation gives you wide scope for all kinds of quirky, interesting arrangements. The partitioning off of small nooks and crannies, but always within the area which

Below: *If you keep your guniea pig in one of the cages illustrated on page 40, make sure you give it plenty of exercise around the house. An open-ended cardboard box makes a convenient bolt hole.*

Above: *Encourage your child to help look after the guinea pig and share the responsibilities of caring for your pet.*

opens into the room, helps create an interesting and a happy home for guinea pigs. Use glass partitions with smooth, bevelled top edges.

This kind of housing is ideal for young families, enabling adults and children to share the joys and responsibilities of caring for animals. It can certainly improve the veterinary care of guinea

A word of warning!

Cover all electrical leads and wires or put them up out of reach, not forgetting any telephone leads in any room in which you plan to let your free-range guinea pigs roam freely. They are particularly partial to telephone cords and may bite through them, cutting off your phone.

CHAPTER
THREE

pigs when children take an interest. Frequently when parents have asked me, in a slightly 'to humour the child' kind of manner, to examine a guinea pig, I have discovered that their child has noticed something about the animal that the adult has missed. Children are very observant and usually spend more time down at guinea pig level than adults. Needless to say, very young children must always be supervised and never left alone with guinea pigs.

Types of indoor accommodation

For owners who lack 'do-it-yourself' skills, there are many types of indoor accommodation that can be bought from most pet stores. Most indoor pens now have plastic bottoms to them and the tops can be made of either wire mesh or plastic.

Above: *This cage has wire sides as a variation on a plastic model. It should not be sited in direct sunlight for any length of time.*

Left: *Plastic cages are ideal for indoor use as they are light and very easy to keep clean.*

Above: *Movable wire mesh arks come in a variety of shapes and sizes but the best ones have one end covered to provide the animal with some shade and shelter from the rain. Alternatively, you can drape a towel over one end.*

Size of pen

The golden rule is the bigger the better. The smallest that I use for my boarders is 70 x 45 cm/28 x 18 in and 45 cm/18 in high for housing two guinea pigs. If the smallest size is used, it is kinder to keep the animals in the room in which you spend the most time and to let them out for a run around each evening.

Exercise and grazing

If you have a garden, particularly a lawn, then movable wire mesh arks are ideal in the summertime for they allow your guinea pigs to graze and enjoy a different exercise area. By moving them about, they will also save you the trouble of mowing the lawn, for guinea pigs can act as excellent 'lawn mowers' and 'fertilizers'. Guinea pig droppings have all the qualities of good horse manure.

CHAPTER
THREE

Housing guinea pigs with rabbits

No matter what you have read, seen on television or have been told in the past, never house a guinea pig with a rabbit. Hundreds of guinea pigs are kicked or suffer injuries and stress when rabbits try to mate with them. This will most certainly happen if they are housed together. Most rabbit fancy organisations are as much against this practice as most dedicated fanciers of guinea pigs. They are well aware of the dangers of feeding rabbits too much green vegetation, whereas the opposite applies in the case of guinea pigs. They are different animals with different needs in their temperament, diet and handling. So for the health and safety of your guinea pigs, don't house them with rabbits — it results only too often in dead or seriously injured guinea pigs.

▌ Bedding

When considering which bedding to use for your guinea pigs, the number-one rule is to never use sawdust or wood shavings. I used to think that this was permissible but I have grown wiser in recent years and am now totally against the practice for the following reasons.

■ There are always fine dust particles in sawdust or wood shavings and as guinea pigs are the type of animals that root around with their noses close to the ground, they breathe in these particles.

■ Although wood shavings may soak up the animals' urine they do not give it a chance to evaporate. Therefore, on grounds of hygiene, they are not a good idea. If you really want to use wood shavings, then use shredded paper instead.

Hay

The ideal bedding is hay, hay and more hay! If hay is bought by the bale, it is cheaper than shavings. It provides comfort as well as vital roughage, and it is essential in enabling the animals to graze constantly and keep those continuously growing teeth in trim. The traditional hunk of wood which, according to so many authorities, has to be provided for a guinea pig to gnaw, is totally useless in my experience. It is ignored after an initial sniff, and many other owners confirm that they get the same reaction from their own stock. Our animals obviously prefer to do the sensible thing and get stuck into all that lovely hay that we so lavishly supply. Tooth problems in

Newspaper

Now for one of the most common questions which is asked about spreading newspaper on the floor of guinea pigs' housing and accommodation: 'My guinea pigs keep chewing the newspaper; will it harm them?' All guinea pigs chew newspaper but provided that they don't read it first, they will come to no harm! So don't worry if your guinea pigs enjoy nibbling the newspaper.

CHAPTER
THREE

A word of caution

Most people put their guinea pigs into a box while they are
mucking out their quarters. However, if you have boars and
sows, then make sure that you clean out the boars first. If you
do it the other way round, the boars will pick up the scent of
the sows left behind in the box and this invariably arouses their
sexual instincts and can lead to trouble between them.

my guinea pigs are a very rare occurrence and this can be
attributed to bedding them down in hay. Any urine passed onto
the newspaper under the hay quickly evaporates.

Mucking out

The newspaper and hay bedding make the labour of mucking
out much easier for you do not get the soggy mess that you get
with shavings or sawdust. You simply roll up the newspaper with
the hay inside it. Always spray right round the edges of the
guinea pigs' quarters with an animal-friendly disinfectant before
putting in fresh newspaper and hay. There are many purpose-
made brands on the market that are suitable for this.

Water supply

Finally, when supplying water, always choose drip-feed water
bottles rather than water bowls. Only use bottles that have a
ball valve at the ends of the spouts. Bottles that have only an
open-ended gravity air lock tend to leak after guinea pigs who
have been grazing on hay leave a strand of it stuck in the
spout after drinking. Once a week, these bottles should be
cleaned thoroughly, including the spout, with a bottle brush.
Use the type of cleaner that is used for human babies' bottles.

Left: After mucking out, use an animal-friendly disinfectant and spray it around all the edges. Make sure the hutch is dry before covering the floor with some newspaper.

Right: After covering the floor of the hutch with several layers of newspaper, put in a deep layer of hay in which your guinea pig will enjoy burrowing.

Left: Put fresh food and water in the hutch before returning your guinea pig to his home. Hide some larger bits of food, such as cucumber and tomato, around the hutch to give your pet something interesting to do.

CHAPTER FOUR

Feeding your guinea pig

Like all animals, guinea pigs have to be cared for on a daily basis and this includes providing fresh food and water. Giving your pet the right food in the correct proportions is the key to good health.

Your guinea pig's good health will depend to a large extent on the food it eats, and therefore it is important that you provide an interesting varied diet (vegetables, hay, dry food and fruit) which is high in essential nutrients.

Diet

Guinea pigs, like their human owners, will be happier and healthier with as varied a diet as possible. There is a wide range of plants — both cultivated and wild — as well as fruit and dry foods that are good for them. Also like us, they have their own individual fads and preferences when it comes to eating and sometimes this runs in packs. My guinea pigs, for instance, will not touch beetroot, although it is an excellent root crop for them, whereas friends of mine say that their guinea pigs cannot get enough of it.

Variety is the key. Be adventurous in what you supply but when it comes to vegetable matter you should not feed your

CHAPTER
FOUR

guinea pig anything that you would not consider sufficiently fresh to eat yourself.

Root crops

Carrots, turnips, swedes, sugar beet and beetroot are the only root crops that guinea pigs will eat. They have a Bugs Bunny-like passion for a good crunchy carrot. In my home, the nightly ritual ringing of the carrot bell, heralding the arrival of this 'precious' fodder, is the highlight of my pack's day and they react enthusiastically, leaping about, some hooking their forepaws over the glass fronts of their pens while others run round in circles, delirious with delight or scrambling over one another.

Above: *With two young babies to feed, this guinea pig is eating succulent cucumber to boost her fluid intake.*

Green vegetables

All guinea pigs need some green vegetable food every day as well as hay and dried food. When I give talks to children in schools about my animals I always ask: 'What do we have in common with guinea pigs, and very few other animals?'

Children seldom get it right but when prompted by asking them what their parents always say when they eat their dinner, they usually chorus in reply: 'Eat up all your greens.'

In essence, anything in the vegetable line that is good for humans is also good for your guinea pigs with a couple of exceptions.

■ Only give lettuce as a treat as it has little food value.

■ Go easy on the spinach as it is rich in oxalic acid which can upset the digestive system of a guinea pig if too much is eaten.

Guinea pigs can be shrewd judges of what is good for them and although, initially, they tuck into lettuce and spinach, they quickly tire of them and usually leave much uneaten.

Guinea pigs need to get their supply of vitamin C via their vegetable diet so when considering how much green food you should feed them each day, the answer is that each animal needs a good handful of grass or two or three leaves of spring greens, cauliflower or whatever vegetable is in season.

Remember that you should always remove any uneaten vegetables after a few hours. Do not leave them to rot away as bad vegetables are a common cause of diarrhoea in guinea pigs.

Suitable green vegetables

Suitable greens for guinea pigs include:

■ Broccoli
■ Brussels sprouts
■ Cabbage
■ Cauliflower leaves
■ Curly kale
■ Purple sprouting broccoli
■ Spring greens

Note: Cauliflower leaves, the parts of the plant that we foolishly throw away, are richer in nutrients and trace elements than the flower part which we eat and which most guinea pigs are not keen on. However, a word of warning: if you are going to feed cauliflower leaves to indoor guinea pigs, remove any uneaten leaves very quickly or by the end of the day the 'old sock' odour is appalling and very hard to eliminate.

CHAPTER
FOUR

Sweetcorn

A word about sweetcorn (corn on the cob). Guinea pigs just love it and it is logical to think that they must be getting some kind of therapeutic benefit from the way in which they tear into the leaves and seem to enjoy the sound of their own munching. Just throw a corn cob into your guinea pigs' pen and watch them playing tug of war with it and attacking it from different angles. They are certainly doing their teeth good for little remains of the leaves, cob and hard stems after a short time.

Above: *Most guinea pigs adore munching a sturdy corn cob. Highly nutritious, it is also good for their teeth.*

Fruit

Fruit is the food that guinea pigs are the most fussy about. While some munch happily into apples, others will take just a couple of mouthfuls or even ignore them completely. However, be aware that some guinea pigs should never eat apples; perversely, they are usually amongst those who adore them! These particular guinea pigs have a weakness in the membranes of the lips which can be damaged by the acid in apples, leaving the underlying tissue open to fungal or bacterial attack. If left untreated, it can spread up as far as the nostrils and into the mouth. The symptoms are hard, dark scabs around the lips, usually starting at the corners. To find out how to treat this, turn to page 107 in the veterinary section. If your guinea pig has this problem, cut apples out of its diet immediately.

Watermelons, honeydew melons and cucumbers are universally liked, pears are less popular, and bananas, tomatoes, and grapes are either loved or loathed. I have yet to see a single guinea pig eat any part of an orange; indeed, mine seem to shy away from them as though they were hemlock.

Suitable fruit

The following fruit can be fed safely to guinea pigs:
- Bananas
- Grapes
- Honeydew melons
- Pears
- Watermelons

Note: Apples are not suitable for all guinea pigs

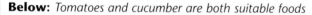

Below: *Tomatoes and cucumber are both suitable foods*

CHAPTER
FOUR

Food from the wild

When foraging in the wild, remember to avoid roadside verges where the flow of traffic is busy as the plants growing there may be affected by car exhaust fumes as well as by passing dogs. As for the foliage itself, keep an eye open for fungal infestation on the leaves which shows up as a white stain, like a tide mark, or as red spotting. Avoid cultivated land also as much of it is contaminated with agricultural chemical sprays at certain times of the year.

The staple wild food for guinea pigs is grass, and lots of it. It is what they have fed upon for thousands of years — rich in vitamin C and fibrous, and therefore excellent for their digestion and their teeth. However, when the first good spring grass comes up, ignore those deep murmurings of contentment and

Below: *Keep an eye on the wild foods that your guinea pig eats. To be on the safe side, check the lists on page 54.*

Above: *Hay provides the best roughage for guinea pigs and should always be freely available.*

appreciative munching when you begin to feed it to them. Although it is their natural food, you have to wean them back on to it gradually, or they may get diarrhoea. Once their digestive systems have adjusted to the rich spring grass, in about a week or so, you can feed them as much as you like throughout the spring and summer.

Grass clippings

A word of warning: never feed mown grass clippings to guinea pigs. If a lawn is all beautiful green grass then it has probably been sprayed with chemicals or some substance that may well be harmful to guinea pigs. However, if it is natural, there may be many other small plants, weeds and mosses growing in it which may be poisonous and are unsuitable for guinea pigs.

CHAPTER
FOUR

Wild plants: good and bad

Suitable wild plants

There are many wild plants that people regard as weeds which
are very good for guinea pigs. These include the following:

- Chickweed (best in early
  spring and late summer)
- Clover (but avoid pink clover)
- Cow Parsley
- Dandelion

- Dock
- Groundsel
- Plantains
- Sow Thistle
- Vetches

Note: Wild plants crop at different times of the year, especially
in the summer, so there should be a plentiful supply for your
guinea pigs all the year round.

Poisonous plants

There is a general rule of thumb which is helpful when making
judgements about the safety of poisonous plants. This states
that plants grown from bulbs, such as bluebells and daffodils,
and evergreens are more likely to be poisonous. Poisonous
plants include the following:

- Anemone
- Belladonna
- Bindweed
- Boxwood

- Buttercup
- Celandine
- Foxglove
- Hemlock

- Rhubarb, wild
  or cultivated
- Potato leaves

When deciding whether to feed wild plants to guinea pigs, the
best rule is if in doubt, leave it out or check up on it.
Organic poisoning, caused by eating a poisonous plant, is
more likely to affect an immature guinea pig than an older
one. However, this kind of poisoning is relatively rare. Nature
has decreed that the majority of these poisonous plants are
unpleasant to taste and they are usually abandoned by guinea
pigs after a tentative nibble.

Dry feedstuffs

The choice of proprietary dry feeds available nowadays is very wide indeed and it is always advisable to stick to these rather than to mix your own. Many people are worried about the additives in dry feeds but there are relatively few and they are usually there for a good reason, such as replacing an element that has been degraded in the processing of the feed. Thanks to a tightening of consumer legislation in many countries, the contents are now clearly marked on the sacks of these dry feedstuffs to allow the customer to make a more informed choice.

Which feed?

When deciding on a feed, it is a good idea to let your guinea pigs make their own choice by trying out a brand, in small trial amounts, and checking to see how much of the mix is eaten at the end of the day. When a new brand appears on the market, you can repeat this procedure and try switching to another brand for a few months.

It is always a false economy to opt for the cheapest you can buy for you will only end up with wasted food if your guinea pigs refuse to eat it. The dry feed that I buy is in the medium-price range but, from my own experience and by speaking to other owners, I have come to the conclusion that the price tag has little relevance to the contents as far as the guinea pigs and their preferences are concerned. The golden rule, of course, is to only feed a choice of brands that contain a wide range of ingredients

ACS additives

Up until a few years ago, many of the mixes of rabbit food had the letters ACS (Anti-Coccidiosis sprayed) on the list. Coccidiosis is more common in rabbits than in guinea pigs, and this kind of sprayed food could harm young guinea pigs. Fortunately, very few of these rabbit mixes are now sprayed, so this has enabled guinea pig owners to have an even wider choice of dry feeds for their pets. Conversely, it has been of benefit to the manufacturers of these rabbit feeds in that it has opened up the guinea pig market to them. However, if you are using rabbit feed, do check the label.

**CHAPTER
FOUR**

and which will give your guinea pigs a healthy, balanced diet.

All the labels on these brands give a protein, oil, fibre and ash content. As I am against over-feeding protein, I always opt for dry feeds at the lower end of the scale which can range from fourteen to eighteen per cent protein. The higher the fibre the better but this doesn't always mean that the fibre content is going to be high in a low-protein feed. So shop around to get the balance that you feel is best for your pet's health and vitality.

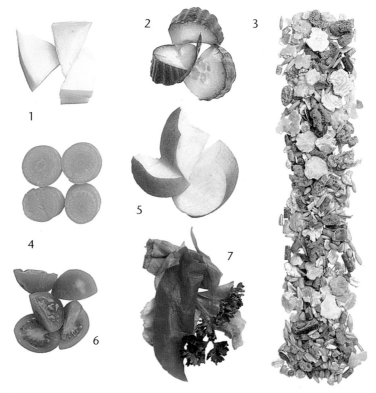

Above: *Pictured here are the main ingredients for a balanced diet for a healthy guinea pig. These include:* **1** *Melon;* **2** *Cucumber;* **3** *Guinea pig mix;* **4** *Carrot;* **5** *Apple;* **6** *Tomato;* **7** *Green vegetables, including parsley and lettuce.*

Wet versus dry feeds

You can get either wet or dry types of feed which means that some have molasses added while others do not. Although there is some debate about the merits of each type of feed, I still allow my guinea pigs to choose which they prefer. I certainly have never found that there are any differences nutritionally in these feeds, and know of no evidence that proves that one is better than the other.

Alfalfa and long-fibre mix

It is a good idea to purchase feed and hay from companies that supply stables, for they also stock two other very important types of fodder for guinea pigs. One is alfalfa by the bale and the other is a long-fibre mix, which is rich in herbs, for horses. Mix in some of the alfalfa with the hay, and a couple of times a week try mixing some of the long-fibre mix with the dry feed.

When to feed and how often

Finally, when should you feed your guinea pigs — and how much? It is always wise to establish a feeding routine and to stick to a set time each day. You could try feeding the vegetable matter first thing in the morning before you have your own breakfast. As soon as your guinea pigs have 'eaten up all their greens' you can top up their dry feed troughs. At about eight in the evening, you could feed them their daily ration of carrots. However, don't follow this slavishly — just work out a routine that suits you and your guinea pigs, but make sure that they always have water and hay and that their dry feed troughs are topped up.

CHAPTER FIVE

Handling and grooming

Guinea pigs are tough, assertive little animals and enjoy being handled. The commonly held idea that they are over-sensitive and prone to throw fits or die of a heart attack if startled is total nonsense, as is the myth that they give up very easily when they are ill and are liable to roll over and die.

The urgency of guinea pig movements when startled is not a design fault but a benefit, for it enables them to take avoiding action when under threat. The guinea pig's highly sensitive nervous system compensates for its inability to fight off a predator. Although domestic guinea pigs are less alert than their wild cousins, the characteristic defence of immediate flight from the unknown is wisely retained in their make-up. It is the 'unknown' that your newly acquired guinea pigs have to get familiar with when they first come to live in your home, and this means you and an unfamiliar environment.

Handling your guinea pigs

The more you handle your guinea pigs, the better it is for both you and them. If guinea pigs are nervous and hyperactive, then it is because their owners have not spent enough time with them and have not handled them enough.

CHAPTER
FIVE

Guinea pigs housed indoors

For the first couple of days in their new home, leave your guinea pigs alone to settle down and to become familiar with their surroundings. However, do not creep about on tiptoe nor should you tell your children to keep quiet during this time. It is best for the new small members of your household to quickly become socialized and accustomed to household noises. They must learn right from the start that although they are now living with noisy humans the noise is not a threat to them. They quickly grasp the fact that they are secure in their own accommodation.

Guinea pigs housed outside

Of course, if your guinea pigs are living outdoors the temptation to pick them up and pet them is less, for they are out of sight for most of the time. Naturally it takes longer for outdoor guinea pigs to settle down. Although I believe that outdoor guinea pigs never become as tame as those housed indoors, nevertheless, they too can become very responsive to gentle handling, and the more of it they get the better.

Mucking out

As mucking out has to take place every two or three days, why not make the first time you have to do it an opportunity to start getting acquainted? Try and make it a family affair so that you can teach your children what to do and get them into the habit of carrying out this essential chore.

Picking up a guinea pig

There is one rule that must be strictly adhered to when children are handling guinea pigs, and this is that very young children should never walk about holding guinea pigs in their arms. Older children must be told always to put one hand firmly over any guinea pig they are carrying.

Guinea pigs are not very keen on heights and although most stay put when they are a few feet above the ground some have a suicidal tendency to suddenly launch themselves out into space. Be warned, aerodynamically, guinea pigs have the gliding qualities of a house brick!

1 When you reach into a guinea pig's quarters to pick one up, it usually runs and buries its head in the nearest corner, presenting you with a broad bottom which is very convenient for slipping the palm of your hand under.

2 Take its weight before you lift, putting your other hand firmly over the back before lifting it out.

3 Occasionally, a guinea pig will back into a corner so slip your hand right under its rump until the trunk is lying on your arm. Put your other hand on top and then lift it out.

CHAPTER
FIVE

This lifting procedure is important because most of the fall injures that are sustained by guinea pigs occur either when they are being lifted out or put back into their quarters. It cost one of my guinea pigs its life and myself much heartache because I did not have a firm enough hold upon it. It fell to the ground, ran a few steps and dropped down dead with a broken neck.

Once the guinea pig is safely settled on your lap, try talking to it, if not in its own langauge, then in the tones of it. Make little clicking sounds with your tongue and purr at it. Ignore any mockers of your efforts to open up a person-to-piggy conversation — your turn will come to get your revenge when your critics do the same thing. Very few people can resist making 'cooing' noises when they pet a guinea pig for the first time. However, most of all be tactile, for guinea pigs are very 'touchy feely' animals.

Restlessness

If the guinea pig simply will not settle at all and constantly strives to get off your lap, then let it go. Although you are bigger and stronger, this is no excuse for imposing your will upon it. Most guinea pigs settle down after a minute or so and enjoy being petted. Those that initially resist petting, usually get used to it in time. It may take weeks or even months, but allow those that want to take their time to do just that. Occasionally, you will get a guinea pig that doesn't like being petted at all; if so, respect its wishes and admire it for being a little on the wild side.

If, after a guinea pig has settled down and has accepted your attentions for a while, it suddenly begins to get restless, be advised to put it down for it has either had enough or it is trying to tell you something which you would be wise to heed. Many times this restlessness is the guinea pig equivalent of raising its hand in class. They seem to show this consideration to their owners right from the first time they are handled. However, they only give notice of

Settling your guinea pig

A great deal of a guinea pig's vocalizing is accompanied by grooming and body-to-body contact. Most like being massaged under the ears or round the back of their necks and some like to be fondled under their lower jaws. Whereas some are putty in your hands when you stroke the tops of their heads, others only like it for a very short time or not at all. They let you know when they don't like being handled or tire of it, in no uncertain terms, by throwing their heads up irritably and pushing your hand away. Some people think that this is cute and continue to touch them, but these are the times when I dearly wish that guinea pigs would be less reluctant to use their teeth to let their feelings be known more forcefully.

their need to relieve themselves when they urinate, for they seem to have no qualms about depositing pellets in their owners' laps. It could have something to do with the fact that they need to lift themselves and squat when they urinate which is much more awkward in a human lap than on firm ground.

CHAPTER
FIVE

Replacing a guinea pig in its quarters

You must be even more fastidious when putting a guinea pig back into its quarters or a carrying box than you were when taking it out. Most guinea pigs have a tendency to leap out of your hand before they are lowered into their home. There are two ways to avoid this, so experiment with the following:

■ You can lower them into the pen or box in reverse.

■ You can cup your hand over their heads if you are lowering them in face first.

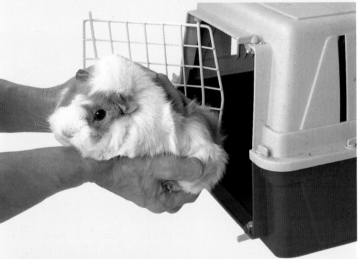

Above: *If your pet does not like being confined,* put it in backwards, cupping it underneath.

Left: *When putting the animal in forwards, cup* its head.

Settle for just a lap petting session the first few times you handle your guinea pigs. The joys of nose and neck nuzzling, nasal gazing, tummy tickling and discovering each guinea pig's soft spots can come later.

Everyday care

The most important kind of care that you can provide for your guinea pigs is to check them out each morning when you feed them. Your eyes are all that are needed for this. The most important health check is to watch the way they go for their first meal of the day. They usually let you know, very vocally, before you even get to put any food into their quarters. Their ecstatic squeaks of appreciation are one of the many pleasures of keeping these animals. In my case, with seventy of the wee beasties, it's more of a morning chorus which swells to a mighty crescendo as I approach with a basket of fresh green stuff.

Despite having such a large number, it is still easy to scan them all and pick out any who are less enthusiastic, so that I can take a closer look. For more information on detailed health checks, turn to page 104. In addition, you must refill all water bottles daily and top up the dry feed troughs or bowls.

Right: *Long-haired guinea pigs, such as the Texel, require more attention and regular grooming than smooth-coated animals.*

CHAPTER
FIVE

▌ Additional care

In addition, all guinea pigs need to be shampooed at three-monthly intervals, and long-haired varieties will need grooming.

Grooming

The only animals that need grooming are the long-haired varieties and even these only need their rear-end hair trimmed every so often to stop them becoming soiled. Cut the rear coat down to ground level, then pull it back up over the back and layer cut it downwards — my guinea pigs have the lower part of their rumps cut down to crew cut proportions. You then just let the scooped hair fall back down into place and the result is that they don't look as though they have been trimmed at all. That and a regular three-monthly shampoo are all that is needed for the animals to look and feel well.

Left: *A 'rag mop' cut is not suitable for show animals.*

Trimming show guinea pigs

Guinea pigs that are destined for the show circuit, particularly the long-haried varieties, must not be trimmed so drastically. As the rules and regulations, particularly about coat textures, lengths and colours, are so detailed they are not covered in this book and you should seek expert advice.

However, some people like to do their own styles, such as a rag mop cut, or trimming the rump right up to the waist. Purists may frown upon this, claiming that it is not 'natural'. In my opinion, this is nonsense. Guinea pigs are not wild animals and they don't have politically correct hang-ups. It does no harm to them and people who indulge their whims in this kind of way invariably handle their animals a great deal, which is of great benefit to the guinea pigs.

Shampooing your guinea pig

Shampooing your guinea pig is an important weapon against many kinds of skin and parasite problems as well as keeping their coats clean and healthy.

■ It is vital that guinea pigs should be shampooed at least once every three months, in spite of their protestations. However, some guinea pigs do appear to enjoy the experience, and if your animals fall into this category it will make the process easier.

■ Use a baby bath or the kitchen sink. Just fill a large jug with warm (not hot) water and pour it over the guinea pig which is sitting in the sink. Use a shampoo that is specially formulated for small animals or a very mild scalp cleansing shampoo which is suitable for humans.

■ Work up a good lather and shampoo the coat all over, not forgetting the face but taking care not to get it into the ears and eyes. Leave the shampoo on for about 5 minutes and then rinse it off with warm water. You can either pour this from a jug or use a hand-held shower attachment fixed to the hot and cold taps.

■ Rub briskly with a towel to dry the guinea pig and then return it to its quarters if it lives indoors. With outdoor animals, wait until they are thoroughly dry.

A note of warning

When grooming the rear ends of boars, be sure to cup their testicles as shown in the photograph. Snicks in the sacks of these vital organs are very common when new and inexperienced owners first groom their guinea pigs.

Grooming procedure

When carrying out any kind of grooming with a brush or comb, make sure that you grasp the animal's coat very firmly close to the skin. Guinea pigs have very sensitive skin and any kind of tugging on the coat hurts them. Be warned that if you don't do it properly, this is one of the rare scenarios where your guinea pig may swiftly turn its head and bite you. Having experienced the full force of those needle-sharp incisor teeth in my thumb when I once tugged too hard, I strongly advise owners to guard against this!

Don't attempt this grooming until you have got your guinea pig really lap-friendly. Some people find it easier to groom their guinea pigs when they have them settled down on a cushion or pillow, either in their laps or on a table. There are no golden rules apart from choosing the method with which you feel most comfortable.

Left: *When grooming your guinea pig, tease out any knots and tangles in the long hair before using a brush or comb.*

Above: The grooming brushes and combs that are made specially for dogs and cats are also suitable for long-haired guinea pigs. Use ordinary nail clippers, which are available from most chemists.

Above: When grooming, use the 'under and over' technique. Gently brush the underside of the coat first and then brush or comb the top side.

Above: Carefully trim the undercoat and then flick the top layer of hair back over the trimmed hair.

Above: Comb through the hair over the rump, remembering to cup the testicles if it's a boar.

CHAPTER
FIVE

▌ Get to know your guinea pigs

As time goes by and your guinea pigs become more familiar with one another, you will quickly get to know their little foibles. You'll learn how to treat them as individuals and how foolish it is to regard them just as pack animals without any character. You can start by having some fun with them.

I have yet to hear of anyone picking up an infection from the kind of close contact behaviour I am about to describe unless the animal has a skin condition. Obviously if this is the case then common sense dictates that you desist until it clears up. There are some people who are allergic to animal fur or hair and therefore they should not try this kind of close contact. Also, of course, only play these games with compliant guinea pigs.

Nose nuzzling

With the guinea pig's head held firmly in the palm of one hand and supporting its trunk with the other, lift it to your face and gently rub noses. You usually get one of the following reactions

from the guinea pig. Either it will gently lick your nose or, with its delicate nose all of a twitch and its big wide eyes peering intensely, it will study your face.

Nasal gazing

Lie on your back with a pillow under the back of your head, and place a guinea pig high up on your chest.

▌ **Left:** *Nasal gazing is enjoyable for both you and your pet.*

Gently blow up at it and await results.
Guinea pigs sometimes purr as soon as you
do this and nearly always twitch their
whiskers. Some will walk forwards, take a
closer look and then put a paw on your
chin and peer at you. Others will simply
just take the weight off their legs, lay their
warm tummies on your chest and lie there
in deep contentment.

Above: *Some guinea pigs enjoy
having their tummy tickled.*

Tummy tickling

This is only for a few guinea pigs, for most
do not like being put onto their backs
and should never be pressured into this
position. Those that do like it invariably
love being cradled in their owners' arms
and having their tummy tickled.

Grooming and bonding

Over the years I have observed the mutual
grooming behaviour of guinea pigs and
have come to the conclusion that this is a
very important part of their bonding with
individual members of the pack. They will

Above: *Nose nuzzling helps
you to get to know each other.*

feel the same kind of bonding with those owners who make the
effort to find out what pleases individual guinea pigs and take
the time to 'groom' them too.

Try and discover where individual guinea pigs like being
stroked or tickled. A general rule is that the further towards the
rump of the guinea pig you go, the less they like it. Have fun
with your guinea pigs but do it on their terms. These captivating
animals enjoy play for play's sake and not just as an exercise in
survival craft.

CHAPTER SIX

Behaviour

In their wild habitat in South America, guinea pigs are naturally pack animals and cohabit together in large groups with relatively little friction. However, domestic guinea pigs rarely live in packs and are more likely to be single or to live in pairs of sows or boars.

As we have seen already, guinea pigs are very adaptable animals and socialize well with each other and with humans. By watching their movements and body language and by listening carefully to the wide range of noises that they make, you can learn more about their behaviour and understand your pet(s) better. Aggression, anger, fear and contentment are all expressed vocally by guinea pigs.

▌Vocalization

Guinea pigs have a vast range of vocalization and I believe that it is the ability of guinea pigs to communicate in this manner that has led to them being such gentle and peace-loving creatures.

In my living room I have forty sows (females) living together in a very long pen and serious in-fighting simply does not occur. The occasional head or chin butt, the shoulder shove or back kick are not meant or taken seriously. If tempers do get heated then this is when the vocabulary comes into play. Guinea pigs seem to settle their differences sensibly with 'jaw, jaw, jaw rather than war, war war.'

CHAPTER
SIX

Most other pack aninals, particularly carnivores, do have vocal as well as body language but they are are usually far more aggressive than guinea pigs, slipping into flared nostrils, raised hackles and bared teeth mode with very few preliminaries.

Although boar guinea pigs (males) can be more aggressive than females, most of them are reluctant to fight when they are first put together. There is a set ritual that has to be gone through before combat between guinea pigs. The time that it takes to perform this ritual may vary and some of it sometimes gets cut short. By describing it, we can encompass the three basic sounds with which guinea pigs communicate. They are the purr, the squeak and the throat moan.

The purr

This can be subdivided into three with a couple of minor variations:

■ The purr of contentment when being groomed by other guinea pigs or their owners is a cosy, quiet and spontaneous sound that seems to be more instinctive than contrived.

■ The amorous purr is more vibrant and, naturally enough, sensuous and invariably is accompanied by body swaying and hip twitching.

■ The purr of aggression simply sounds like a growling purr, and much louder than the other two purrs described. This is usually, but not always, accompanied by pacing on the spot with the back feet.

Left: *Guinea pigs are naturally inquisitive and like to explore. New objects have to be sniffed.*

The squeak

There are many kinds of squeak and they can cover the whole range of emotions.

■ The most common kind of squeaking is what can only be described as conversational. You will hear it in the background quite often, like a buzz of conversation whenever guinea pigs are gathered together in groups. This squeak is pitched low and is as likely to come in short bursts as singly.

■ The squeak of annoyance is much louder, a little higher in pitch and more staccato and sometimes comes at a stutter.

■ The squeak of alarm or anger is way up in the guinea pig's decibel range, and is probably designed to frighten off predators and warn the rest of the pack of danger. A wild screech would probably be a better description of it.

■ There is also a kind of interrogatory squeak which a guinea pig makes when it is unsure of a place or situation. It will make this sometimes before entering a room if there is something new in it. It will stand in the doorway, sniffing the air, peering intently while it decides whether it is safe to enter.

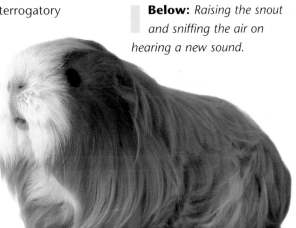

Below: *Raising the snout and sniffing the air on hearing a new sound.*

The throat moan

If you have ever heard a child whining because he doesn't want something or is being denied something, then this is the sound of the throat moan. It is most commonly heard when one guinea pig 'wants to be alone' while another wants to snuggle up to it.

Other sounds and behaviour

One of the most appealing sounds is the 'hut, hut, hut' that
some guinea pigs make when they are exploring new quarters or
simply just walking around the house. In Gavin Maxwell's
wonderful book, *Ring of Bright Water*, he says that otters make
the same sound when they enter a room.

Ritual behaviour

Now for the ritual that can lead to combat but can also very often
prevent it. If after the preliminary sniffing of both front and back
ends, when two guinea pigs who are strangers to one another
meet, there is the long, low growling purr, then don't leave the
animals alone and have a towel ready to hand. If the purr
becomes more vibrant and slips into the throat moan, stand by.

The next stage is either the characteristic slow pacing of the
back feet of either one or both animals and a kind of ducking and
weaving of the heads of the combatants. This
is soon followed by raising the hackles on
the back of their necks.
Heads are held

high and the mouths open to show their powerful incisor teeth, in threatening mode.

When they begin to castanet their teeth and pull back a little to give themselves more room to launch an attack, this is the time to throw the towel over the pair of them. This confuses them and as they feel more under threat from the darkness and the feel of the towel on their bodies than from the other guinea pig, they always break off the engagement. Never ever put your hand in to try and part them — it hurts!

There is a very good reason for not intervening earlier. It is that usually one or both will break off the engagement before it reaches the critical stage. After all, the ritual is designed to defuse potential hostility and conflict. When this happens and one breaks off and turns away, the other will seldom press the matter.

Feeding time

The squeak of joy when food is about to descend from above is unmistakable for it is usually backed up with lots of leaping as the guinea pigs tumble over one another in a frenzy of excitement.

Below: Guinea pigs are naturally pack animals and a group of sows will live happily together.

It seems to be the case that there is no
kudos to be gained by pursuit
after the exchange of verbal
and body language.
It is far better
for guinea pigs
to sort these
things out for
themselves than
have their owner
intervene,
particularly if this occurs
within a pack where most of these disputes amount to
nothing more than sorting out the pecking order.

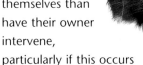
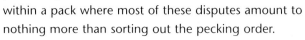

There is another threat sign which can happen after one of
these skirmishes or as a way of preventing them. It is a very
prolonged 'in your face' yawn which one guinea pig will give to
another that it thinks needs to be reminded of the size of its
powerful incisor teeth.

The golden rule is to persevere if you have two guinea pigs
which are aggressive towards one another, for they will usually
settle down after a while. However, once blood is drawn on
either side, you must house them separately.

Some sound variations

■   A 'Drrr' sound is usually made in response to new sounds
that are not considered threatening. A good example is when a
visitor's mobile phone rings. Your guinea pigs will be accustomed
to the ringing of the house phone and know it is benign but
they will not recognise the noise of the mobile and may emit a
'Drrr' as an exclamation of puzzlement.

■   The 'murmur' sound which comes from the back of the throat
signifies deep contentment or delight. This could be triggered by

fresh spring grass or cucumber, or when the guinea pig is being stroked or groomed. It's an alternative way of showing their appreciation rather than using the more common purr. It may also be made when two guinea pigs snuggle up together.

The guinea pig's 'song'

The 'chrripup' or, as some people call it, 'the song' is one of the unanswered questions about guinea pig behaviour. Unless someone is in the room or close by when it begins and can home in on it, their immediate reaction is that a bird has become trapped inside the guinea pig's quarters for it sounds just like the 'peep, peep, peep' of a small bird.

Although this is a very well known phenomenon, many people who have kept guinea pigs for years have never witnessed it. This may be because they have not been living with them. Having lived with so many guinea pigs for such a long time, I have seen and heard this strange behaviour many times.

At first there is a short, sharp panting of breath — 'ha, ha, ha, ha!' — and then gradually the vocal chords are brought into play. At this stage, all other guinea pigs in the vicinity will freeze. From then on, there is an ethereal quality about the performance. The guinea pig making the noise usually raises its head high and gives the appearance of being in a trance-like state. Its companions will either look towards it or stand transfixed, staring ahead. It can last for a minute or carry on for a few minutes.

Sometimes it stops abruptly with the guinea pig giving a shake of its head and looking a little confused. Alternatively, it will gradually tail off and just continue as if nothing unusual had occurred. Sometimes, some of the guinea pigs nearest to it will sniff it afterwards, as though checking it to see if it's all right. A theory has been put forward that this behaviour is stress related but invariably, in my experience, it has always occurred in quiet periods when there was no threat or noise.

CHAPTER
SIX

▌ Travelling boxes

I transport my guinea pigs in a long travelling box with small guinea-pig sized compartments. In this way, I can take up to four animals with me at a time and my 'passengers' feel secure. I was once taken to task about the small compartments in my travelling box. I pointed out that when an animal such as a guinea pig was frightened it always sought out a small hidey hole and this is just what I provide for mine as they experience the bumping

Above: *Cardboard boxes are fine for short-term use when transporting guinea pigs.*

and noise which many trips involve. The bonus is that they are not likely to suffer bruising or broken limbs in a car that brakes suddenly as might happen if they tumbled about in a larger compartment. This is an important point to consider when transporting guinea pigs in the normal-sized travelling cases. Always pack them very firmly with hay so that in the event of accidents the occupants cannot be thrown about inside the box.

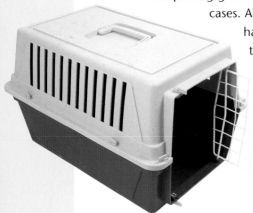

Left: *Plastic travelling cases are more sturdy and last longer.*

Zoonoses

This a fancy word for describing the kind of diseases that can be passed from animal to human. The guinea pig is particularly people-friendly in this respect. Apart from a fungal skin condition to which guinea pigs can be prone (see pages 110-111), they do not pose any threat to human health.

If your guinea pigs begin to show any signs of a skin condition, then don't let your children handle the pets until they have been properly diagnosed and treated.

For the past ten years I have been visiting the young patients at Great Ormond Street Childen's Hospital in London with my guinea pigs. Neither I, nor the hospital staff, have had the slightest worry about these animals being a health hazard to the children. Needless to say, each one gets a rigorous veterinary check on the morning of our visits and any with the slightest sign of a skin condition stay at home.

If anyone had any doubts about the people friendliness of these animals, then a trip with my guinea pigs on one of my weekly hospital visits would dispel them. I have to add that many of the staff and parents of the patients have quickly become ardent fans as a result of the way the guinea pigs behave when being handled by children. That it is good therapy for the children there can be little doubt. As for the staff, their enthusiasm for these weekly visitors is as great as those of their charges.

CHAPTER SEVEN

Breeding

Breeding must be undertaken responsibly. Unfortunately, far too many people breed guinea pigs without serious thought about what will happen to the young after the euphoria of birth and weaning wears off.

deally, owners should only breed from animals if they plan to keep the young themselves or have arranged for them to be homed by friends who also own guinea pigs and are aware of their needs. The responsiblity for guinea pigs should not end with the animals you own but should also extend to their young.

In-breeding

The number one rule when considering breeding is never to in-breed. Mother Nature has been in the business for a long time and we should follow her example. She determined that in-breeding was not permissible by ensuring that when the male guinea pigs that live in packs reach the age at which they become fertile they are hounded out of the immediate family group to prevent them breeding with their relations. In-breeding can cause physical deformities, weaken the body's immune system and shorten the animal's life span.

Breeds that should never be bred together are Dalmatians and Roans. If these breeds are required, then breed by carrier: breed the pure-bred guinea pig with some other cross breed to get a good varied mixture of the genes. More often than not,

CHAPTER
SEVEN

one or two of the young produced will be a carrier of the breed you like. You can then breed it with the pure breed of your choice but not, of course, related to its mother or father.

Ideal age for breeding

Never breed a guinea pig which is over twelve months of age unless it has already given birth to a brood earlier in its life. There is more likelihood in older guinea pigs of them suffering from dystocia, a condition which prevents the pubic bones from parting properly to allow passage of the young, or pregnancy inertia when they are bred late.

The ideal age for breeding is five to six months and although sows of four years of age can have a brood quite successfully I always think that one should stop at three years.

Gestation period

The gestation period is between sixty-three and seventy-five days. This seems like a wide margin and it is due to two reasons:
- It is very hard to determine the exact date of conception.
- There are so many factors that can shorten or lengthen the pregnancy. Minor illnesses during pregnancy and spells of extreme weather conditions are the main considerations that affect the length of pregnancies.

Gynaecological problems

Guinea pigs that have been bred from, even just once, tend to suffer less from gynaecological problems. However, this does not mean that all sows that do not have litters are going to suffer these problems. As most of these problems can be treated successfully, breeding as an insurance against them occurring is not justifiable.

Health checks

Before you put a sow and boar together, carry out a health check (see the chart on page 104). If possible, try and find out if there have been any problems with the offspring of the sow or boar if they have been bred before. If there have been, it is wise to think again before breeding as there is a risk of genetic problems coming through. They will not necessarily happen, and indeed many times when a guinea pig with a 'fault' has been mated with another partner the problem is eliminated. Therefore, don't get overly concerned if you find out after the mating has taken place that there has been a problem in a previous litter sired or carried by either partner.

A sow has an oestrus cycle of fifteen to seventeen days. Although she is sexually active for between twenty-four and forty-eight hours, the oestrus (the period when she can conceive) lasts only for between two and eleven hours.

If you are planning to breed from your guinea pigs, you would be advised to keep the pair together for at least six weeks

Right: *This heavily pregnant sow is fast approaching her due date.*

and that way you can be sure of catching the sow's cycle twice. In my experience, at least fifty per cent of the sows I have paired have not conceived in their first season with the boar.

Choosing a sow or boar

The deciding factor when choosing a particular sow or boar from which to breed is their temperament. This does not mean that you should rule out a boar or sow which is, say, more scatty or less amenable to human handling. If either prospective mate does not have the kind of temperament you like but its looks or breed appeals to you, then breed it with a guinea pig which does have the desired qualities in temperament.

▌Courting behaviour

Although there are a few boars who do not chase the sow around, most will try to mate her as soon as they are put in with her. The sow usually squeaks and makes a lot of noise but this is not a

Below: *Most sows accept the boar's attentions.*

Hair loss

Never breed if either animal shows any signs of hair loss for this could be evidence of a parasitic or fungal problem. If it's the boar that has the problem, he is liable to pass it onto the sow. If it's the sow, it is not wise to treat her during pregnancy as some remedies could cause harm to the developing foetuses. Sows with either parasitic or fungal problems can easily pass them on to their young within the womb.

The most common genetic problems are maloccluded teeth, under-shot jaws and, less commonly, cleft palettes. Deformed or in-turned feet do occasionally occur but some of the latter can be caused by the way the young were carried in the womb and can be corrected by manipulating the feet during the first week or so after birth; consult your vet.

cause for alarm on the owner's part. Sows have a very effective deterrent when they feel that the boar's attentions have lasted for longer than they are prepared to tolerate. They suddenly put on an extra spurt of speed, then come to an abrupt halt and lift their rumps up in the same way as they do when they are presenting themselves to a boar for mating. The boar, thinking that he has at long last persuaded the sow of her luck in having such a handsome mate as himself, will pause for a brief second to sniff before mounting and be rewarded with a jet of hot urine right up his nostrils. The effect is absolutely devastating and dampens the boar's ardour instantly. He will sit, splutter, sneeze and paw his snout. Sows seldom have to repeat this procedure.

Occasionally a sow will simply not accept a particular boar. This is the one occasion when the preliminaries which usually lead up to combat are dispensed with and she will simply attack him, hackles raised and teeth gnashing. Boars rarely if ever respond in kind. Whether it is because there is some kind of guinea pig etiquette which prohibits offering violence to the opposite sex, or because the boar is simply surprised at the ferocity of the sow, we don't know. Take the boar out and try again with another one a couple of days later. In most cases the sow will accept a different boar.

Occasionally after mating, you will find a small white wax plug in the bottom of the sow's quarters. This is formed within the sow after a successful mating and is designed to seal her vagina to prevent the semen from flowing out. Because this has become dislodged it does not necessarily mean that the sperm has not reached its target but it does make pregnancy a little less likely. Normally, in most matings, this wax plug simply melts away after a while.

If you observe a great deal of sexual activity between the pair, make a note of the dates when it occurs. You will then be able to calculate more accurately when you expect the sow to litter down.

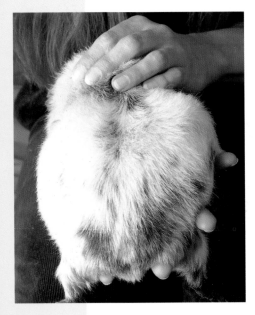

▌ Pregnancy

As soon as you are sure that a sow is pregnant, you could put her on one Raspberry Leaf tablet daily and 0.5 ml of a calcium supplement three times a week to build up her reserves for the task ahead. Do not exceed these doses, which are relatively small and should be regarded just as a small booster.

Left: *Hold a pregnant sow in your palm by splaying your fingers to support the enlarged abdomen. Place a steadying hand on top.*

Signs of pregnancy

The most common signs of pregnancy are listed below:

■   The first indication that a sow has conceived is that you will notice that she is beginning to drink a little bit more than usual. This usually occurs about three weeks after conception.

■   Between three and four weeks there is a firming up of the abdomen and flanks as her muscles begin to tone up for the task to come and some weight is usually gained.

Note: Be aware that there are some sows that can show these signs and not be pregnant. Phantom pregnancies only occur when a sow has been running with a boar.

■   You never know for certain that a sow is pregnant until you can feel the small foetuses, which is usually between four and five weeks into her term. Once it has been established that she is pregnant then there is nothing to be gained by constantly palpating her, trying to find out how many young she is carrying or how big they are getting. This amounts more to idle curiosity rather than serving any useful purpose.

Right: *To feel the 'quickening' of the young in late pregnancy, sit quietly and cup the sow's abdomen gently between your finger and thumb.*

CHAPTER
SEVEN

Hair loss during pregnancy

Loss of hair is not a problem if it begins about halfway through the pregnancy. This is usually indicative of an hormonal imbalance. It is relatively common in all mammals and it is rare for this kind of hair loss to be related to the parasitic and fungal problems described earlier in this chapter. However, if you are worried, ask your vet for advice.

If the sow usually lives with another one, then put her back in with her as soon as the pregnancy is confirmed. If she is a lone sow, then the boar can stay with her until about a week before she is due to litter down. Boars will not harm their young intentionally, but as the sow comes into season a short time after she has given birth, her young could be trampled as the boar tries to mount her.

From now on, it is simply a watching and waiting game. You should avoid handling the sow as much as possible and when it is necessary to lift her out of her quarters when mucking out, splay the fingers of the hand that goes under her to give full support to her greatly increased girth.

Monitoring the sow

You will begin to feel a 'quickening' movement of the young within the sow two to three weeks before she is due to litter down. You don't have to lift her out to feel this; just lean into her quarters and cup your hands on either side of her flanks and hold them there for a short time. However, if she is sensitive, and some sows do become very highly strung when they get close to their time, leave her alone.

The closer she gets to her estimated delivery date the more she should be monitored. In most cases there are no problems but when they do occur it is important that action is taken as early as possible. The signs to look for are:

- Listlessness
- Dribbling at the mouth
- Discharge from the vagina

If you observe any of these warning signs you should take the sow to your vet immediately and get her checked professionally. Expert assistance at this stage could prevent problems occurring later on.

Preparing for birth

The opening of the pelvic bones, in preparation for birth, will sometimes occur over the course of a day or so but not always. Often they become fully open within a few hours. Once they are fully open, which is 1.25 cm/½ inch, then littering down usually begins within forty-eight hours.

CHAPTER
SEVEN

Littering down

For many owners, the first they know of the event is when they go to feed the sow first thing in the morning and find her with a brood tucked up under her. Littering down is more likely to take place at night than during the day. This can be frustrating from the owner's point of view if they have some expertise in basic obstetrics care and the sow has difficulties giving birth.

The grunt that a sow makes when she is experiencing her first contractions is unmistakable, for this is the only time that this kind of grunt is heard. There is a throatiness about it and it can be long drawn out. She will be high on her haunches with legs slightly splayed. Her head will go down between her legs as soon as she feels that the body of her first baby has travelled down the birth canal and its snout is sticking out of her vagina. She will then pull it out by locking her incisor teeth over it, thereby usually breaking the amniotic sac. It is vital that the baby remains in the sac until it is out in the air and ready to take its first breath.

Breech births

Like all mammals, sometimes a sow can have a breech birth which means that the baby is presented bottom or side on. Many breech babies are stillborn for the sacs are usually broken and the young have died due to lack of air. If the baby is blocking the birth canal and cannot be removed, then it is vital that the sow is taken to a vet with known expertise in small animal care. Ask him/her to try and manoeuvre and turn the baby so that it can be delivered normally before deciding on a Caesarean section. This cannot be expected to be successful if too much time has elapsed from the beginning of the labour and the sow has become exhausted. Speed is of the essence here so do not delay in seeking professional medical help.

Above: *These baby guinea pigs are only half an hour old but already their eyes are wide open.*

Sometimes the sac is not properly broken but this is seldom the case for long as the mother always concentrates her efforts on vigorous cleaning of the head in these cases. The sac, which is thin and transparent, like a sausage skin, quickly rolls back over the shoulders of the baby or splits and slips off completely.

Once she is satisfied that the airways are clear, which is sometimes heralded by a slight cough, sounding very much like that of a small human baby's, the mother relaxes a little, becomes more leisurely and begins to work her way all over her firstborn, licking it clean. This licking may also serve the purpose of stimulating the baby to become more active.

CHAPTER
SEVEN

Invariably, her work is interrupted by another contraction as the next of her brood begins to make its entry into this living, breathing world. Most baby guinea pigs are born in quick succession.

Sometimes, two babies can come out together, the second one tumbling out immediately after the mother has pulled the next in line. This one usually still has the sac intact and can be at risk. It depends on how long it takes the mother to deal with the one she pulled out first. The longer it is, the more likely the second one will be in danger of suffocation. By the time she gets the sac off it can be very weak and not be making any effort to get up. This is when she starts playing football with it! She paws and kicks with her forepaws, very roughly, and her movements are much more urgent, as though she knows she is now dealing with an emergency. As soon as the baby coughs or she seems to be satisfied that the airways are clear, she immediately drops back down a gear and the urgency of her movements decreases. One of the striking things about a mother guinea pig giving birth is the methodical matter of factness of her movements. This is why the sense of urgency when things go wrong is so noticeable. It is the equivalent of what the old-fashioned midwives used to do when they lifted a baby up by its ankles and slapped its back to clear the airways.

Opposite: *These three-day-old guinea pigs bed down and suckle happily on their mother's nipples.*

CHAPTER
SEVEN

▌ When to intervene

Sometimes human intervention can be a life saver. If you are present and you see a double birth and one baby is in trouble, do not hesitate to intervene. The mother does not always get there in time and, unlike many animals who are giving birth, there is absolutely no danger that she will resent your assistance or turn upon the baby you have 'midwived'.

1 Pick the baby up and nip the sac by the snout with your fingernails.

2 If it coughs and gets up onto its feet then it's fine, but if it just lies there, cup it in both hands with its head towards your fingertips.

3 Stand up, hold your arms out and swing them through an arch of 160 degrees, vigorously. The centrifugal force this puts upon the baby is usually enough to clear the airways.

4 Alternatively, jiggle it about in your hands, or lay it on its back and pedal its back legs. One of these methods invariably works.

5 As soon as it is up on all-fours, put the baby back under its mother and she will accept it and begin cleaning it.

Weaning the young

The weaning of the young is straightforward. They will suckle from their mother for the first four to six weeks, and they should start to nibble at the same food that their mother is eating within two days of being born. For further information on weaning problems and pregnancy, see Chapter Eight on basic veterinary care.

Although most male guinea pigs do not reach puberty until between eight and ten weeks of age, they should always be removed from the family group by six weeks for there are some that reach puberty much earlier. If the young boars tend to fight a lot among themselves, you may find it helpful to segregate them in different pens.

Above: *Baby guinea pigs grow up fast and soon become independent.*

CHAPTER EIGHT

Basic healthcare

Although the list of ailments that may afflict guinea pigs may look formidable, you should bear in mind that most guinea pigs will only fall victim to one or two of the minor ones. I believe that veterinary knowledge should be far more widely available to owners so that they can help prevent some common health problems occurring in their animals and know how to treat some of the minor ones.

Biological data

Normal body temperature	38.6°C (101°F)
Heart beats per minute	280
Normal respiration rate	80 per minute
Weight: adult boar: adult sow:	900–1180 g (32–42 oz) 860–900 g (30–32 oz)
Birth weight	57–85 g (2–3 oz)
Litter size	2–3 first litter; 3–6 subsequent litters
Life span	5–7 years
Light requirement	10–12 hours

A word of warning: adverse reactions

Always check the droppings and demeanour of a guinea pig when introducing any new medicine or, indeed, food. Anything recommended in this book will have been tried and tested over the years, but, as is the case in human medicines, occasionally one that is brilliant for ninety-nine per cent of patients will provoke an adverse reaction in an individual animal. If there is a problem, then stop the medication immediately.

COMMON MEDICAL CONDITIONS

The following conditions are not serious and rarely need any treatment. However, if you are worried, there is no harm in consulting your vet for reassurance.

Fatty eye

This condition is seen more often in elderly guinea pigs but can sometimes appear in younger ones too. The muscle of the lower eyelid, and occasionally the upper one also, bulges outwards. It is not known what causes this condition in guinea pigs but it does not give those who have it any discomfort or pain. Treatment is not necessary.

Bald patches behind the ears

All guinea pigs have these to a lesser or greater degree. They are more noticeable in Abysinnian breeds because of the configuration of the whirls in their coats.

Towel wrapping

Before attempting to tackle any kind of basic veterinary care, the gentle art of towel wrapping a guinea pig must be perfected. It prevents the animal from becoming stressed during any examination, makes it much easier to control and thereby gives you more time to check the health of your guinea pig. It is nothing more nor less than wrapping the animal up like a babe in swaddling clothes. As the most basic examination should begin by looking into the mouth, ears and eyes, make sure that the front legs are well tucked into the folds of the towel. It is amazing how much strength there is in the front legs and they can soon wriggle out once they have gained leverage against the edges of the towel. By the time you have worked your way down to examine the rest of the animal, it usually feels relaxed. Guinea pigs feel more secure in the folds of the towel than if they are just standing or lying on a plain surface.

▌Heaving hiccups

These cause much alarm when inexperienced owners see them for the first time. The animal appears to be heaving, prior to vomiting. The whole body is rocked and the retching comes from way down below the diaphragm. It usually stops abruptly when the guinea pig gives a little cough.

CHAPTER
EIGHT

Guinea pigs cannot vomit; in essence anything that goes in the front end can only exit by the back. As hiccups usually happen during or just after a guinea pig has eaten, it is simply a matter of something having gone down the wrong way. Think of the way we cough and splutter when we eat too quickly and you will immediately identify with the animal.

Anal impaction

Guinea pigs, like rabbits and some other herbivores, are coprophagic, which means that they reingest some of the pellets they excrete as part of their normal digestion. This is what guinea pigs are usually doing when they can be seen with their heads down between their back legs. These pellets are softer than the ones you see lying about the quarters, and in elderly boars, and occasionally in young ones, they sometimes congeal into a ball in their perianal sacs. The cause is not known; it may be a weakness in the muscles that push and present the pellets.

There is no cure and provided that the owner expels these impacted lumps on a regular basis the boar will be fine. This is best done by holding the boar over the lavatory, legs apart, and pushing the ball out from behind. Sometimes some water-soluble lubricant can help. If in doubt, ask your vet.

Alopecia

This is seen only in elderly sows and in pregnant guinea pigs. If an elderly sow's hair thins but there are none of the symptoms associated with parasitic or fungal skin problems and she does not scratch a lot, then it is most likely to be alopecia, brought on by a hormonal imbalance. Sometimes, after a month or so, the hair will return but in the majority of cases sows stay like this for the rest of their lives. Your sow may not look as pretty as she was in the flower of her youth but it is not a threat to her overall health and there is no effective treatment.

Barbering

Barbering is the practice whereby guinea pigs chew their own hair or one another's. Often one particular adult guinea pig will do this for a certain period of time to its companions and then stop. Only once have I known a guinea pig to repeat this behaviour later in life. Amazingly, although they ingest a great deal of hair, they do not appear to suffer from hair balls.

Cataracts

Abysinnian guinea pigs are more prone to cataracts but all other breeds can get them too. They do not make the guinea pig blind but they do reduce its vision. The cause is unknown and there is no cure.

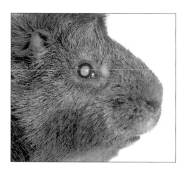

Above: *It is not known why Abysinnians are more prone to cataracts than other breeds.*

Left: *The cataract only covers the iris and both eyes are usually affected.*

CHAPTER
EIGHT

BASIC VETERINARY CARE

Owners should be encouraged to monitor their guinea pigs' health and to take on basic preventative care themselves. 'The earlier the diagnosis, the better the prognosis' is the golden rule, so keep an eye on your pets and take action as soon as you spot the warning signs of potential health problems. Most healthcare amounts to nothing more than common sense and utilizing skills that most parents use to diagnose and treat their own children. However is essential that you seek out a veterinary surgeon who has known skills in treating small animals and, once found, that you recommend him/her to other guinea pig owners.

■ Coat
The coat should not be greasy and, if long haired, it should be free of any tangles and knots. Bald patches, thinning hair or broken hair shafts usually indicate a parasitic problem. If there is deep scurfing, pull a few hairs out. Skin debris attached to the roots may be caused by a fungal condition, possibly combined with a parasitic one.

■ **Ears**
The flaps should be smooth, not scurfy.
A small amount of waxing inside the ear
is perfectly normal, but it should be
cleaned out if it is excessive. This is
seldom an indication of ill health, rather
a lack of human care.

■ **Eyes**
The eyes should be bright
and alert with no sign of
discharge or cloudiness.

■ **Nose**
There should be no sign of
mucus around the nostrils.

■ **Mouth and teeth**
The mouth should be clear
of any scabbing which
can result from a fungal
infection, particularly at the
corners. The incisor teeth
should be white with the
lower ones slightly longer
than the upper ones. If the
teeth impinge at an angle,
there may be problems
with the molar teeth.

■ **Paws**
Check the pads for any calluses
or spurs. These are not indicative
of ill health but the spurs should
be trimmed regularly. Check the
digits are straight and supple.

■ **Skin**
On light-coated guinea pigs which have pink skins,
look out for a deep red hue to the skin which could
mean that there is a fungal problem already there
or one developing. Scurfiness on the skin can be
indicative of fungal or parasitic skin conditions.

CHAPTER
EIGHT

TREATABLE MEDICAL CONDITIONS

▮ Dental and mouth problems

If your guinea pigs get plenty of work to do with their teeth, and they will do if you give them lots of hay and grazing food, dental problems can be kept to a minimum. However, some guinea pigs, who are off their food through illness, can have problems with over-grown incisors and molars. It is no good just trimming the incisor teeth as the molars must be attended to as well. Do not attempt to trim the teeth yourself.

■ Symptoms
The symptoms to look out for are as follows:
- Weight loss
- Dribbling
- Difficulty in chewing

Look carefully at the way the incisor teeth impinge. If they are slanting when looked at face on, then there is a problem or a developing one.

Treatment: There are no nerves in a guinea pig's teeth and therefore any routine corrective dental work should always be carried out without an anaesthetic. Usually, by the time the problem is diagnosed the guinea pig is not fit enough to survive a general anaesthetic. So if this problem occurs, seek out a vet who will carry out this work without anaesthesia.

Note: Get the teeth checked if the guinea pig has ever suffered an abscess in the jaw area for this can cause it to favour the side opposite the site of the abscess, causing the teeth to grow unevenly.

Mouth infections

These can be caused by slightly maloccluded teeth which are not serious enough to affect chewing but can cause ulcers which can become infected by fungus or bacteria. One of the most effective treatments for this condition is to use an oral gel specially formulated for the use of thrush in babies, another fungal problem.

Right: *Guinea pigs actually like the taste of most oral gels.*

Treatment: Just squeeze a small amount of the oral gel into the mouth three times a day during the first week, twice a day for the second week and once daily for the third week. Most guinea pigs recover if they are treated early enough. When the infection has cleared up, feed the guinea pig plenty of green foods with diuretic qualities. If in doubt, consult your vet.

Lip sores

These are often caused by feeding apples to a guinea pig that has a weakness in the membranes of the lips.

Treatment: An effective treatment is to apply Gentian violet daily, and then to pick off the scabs. The lip sores usually clear up within one week. Alternatively, see your vet.

CHAPTER
EIGHT

Did you know?

Unlike dogs, guinea pigs are more likely to sniff one another's ears than their rear ends when they meet for the first time. Others make a beeline for a spot just under each other's chins.

Abscesses

These are quite common around and under the jaws of a guinea pig and most are easy to treat for they are in the skin tissue. Abscesses in the jaw bone are very rare and far more difficult to treat.

Treatment: If your pet has this problem consult your vet who will lance the abscess and carry out any minor kind of surgery required.

Ear problems

These are relatively rare and most can be treated by over-the-counter ear drops which can be purchased at pet shops. If the guinea pig shakes its head a lot and scratches its ear, then it is likely to be an ear mite problem. The best way to prevent this is to keep the ear clear of excessive wax which these mites like to feed upon.
■ If there is a tilt to the head, palpate around the ear; if the guinea pig flinches to the touch, then it probably has an infection.

Treatment: Take the guinea pig to the vet so that the appropriate drug treatment can be prescribed.

Eye injuries

These are quite common and are mainly caused by foreign bodies in the eye or by poke injuries from hay.

■ **Symptoms**

Usually the first indication may be a running eye with the lid half-closed. If these symptoms go unnoticed in the early stages, after a while the whole surface of the eye becomes milky and opaque.

Treatment: Often a hay husk can be seen at the corner of the eye and just needs to be gently removed and the eye flushed with saline solution or any of the proprietary brands of eye washes formulated for humans which are safe to use on guinea pigs. Ask your vet if you are unsure.

Poke injuries

In the case of poke injuries, you can usually see a scratch on the surface of the eye. Generally, these heal completely within a relatively short time without causing any problems to the guinea pig's vision.

Treatment: Use the same method as for foreign bodies in the eye (above). If there is the slightest sign of an infection, such as bulging of the eye, redness and tenderness around it, you must consult your vet immediately so that he can prescribe the correct drug treatment. If left untreated, the infection can be life threatening. The opaqueness usually clears after a few days.

CHAPTER
EIGHT

Blocked tear ducts

Sometimes one of the tear ducts which drain at the front of the eye can become blocked. The eye will water as the natural saline fluid which constantly cleans the surface cannot drain away and thus overflows the eye lid.

Treatment: If you suspect that your guinea pig has a blocked tear duct, it is best to consult your vet who will probably prescribe some eye drops. They are easily applied if the guinea pig is towel-wrapped first (see page 101). If both eyes water, it is usually a sign of general ill health and your pet will need a thorough health check.

Skin problems

Guinea pigs are very prone to skin problems but usually they can be cured easily if they are properly diagnosed and treated. They are caused by either fungal or parasitic infestation, sometimes both.

■ Symptoms

There are differing symptoms for fungal and parasitic skin conditions. Look for the following:

■ If there is a thick, crusty scurf on the skin and the hair comes out in clumps with small white bits on the end of the hair shafts, then it is a fungal problem.

■ If the hair is just thinning or there are bald patches and broken hair shafts, the problem is parasitic.

If you act as soon as the symptoms appear, you can treat both conditions effectively and safely yourself. However, if unsure, you should consult your vet.

Treatment: Conventional treatment for fungal infections is by the use of an anti-fungal dip. This is only available on prescription and can be purchased over the counter at your vet's surgery. A fungal shampoo is another product and can be obtained from stable suppliers. Dip for five minutes, or shampoo and leave on for five minutes, then rinse off. Repeat in three days' time and again after ten days.

Alternative treatment: This is by massaging an anti-fungal oil formula into the animal's skin. Leave for twenty-four hours before shampooing. Repeat after three and ten days. Use the following formula:
• One part patchouli, tea tree, lavender and lemon grass essential oils
• Ten parts carrier oil, e.g. sunflower oil
Therefore, if you take 0.5 ml of each of the essential oils, making a quantity of 2 ml, you will need 20 ml of carrier oil to dilute the formula.
Note: If a guinea pig has been allowed to reach the stage where it is having fits and the scurfing is very thick, it will have become infested systemically and will need to be treated by your vet with an appropriate prescribed drug. Do not delay in seeking expert treatment.

Cysts

These are less of a threat to health than abscesses for they are merely pockets of the guinea pig's sebaceous lubricating material which open into the hair follicles or directly onto the skin. This material is soft and waxy, and when one of these cysts is pressed there is no tension in them, unlike an abscess. They can occur almost anywhere on a guinea pig but are more common on its back and rump.

Treatment: They should be lanced and the material expressed as soon as they reach bean size. If they are allowed to get bigger, they can grow very large and will eventually break, leaving a big crater. It is advisable to seek professional veterinary attention.

Bumblefoot (Pododermatitis)

The symptoms are swelling and sometimes ulceration of the pad of the foot. In the early stages it is painful for the animal to walk on, but they seem to adapt to the condition quite well. Although many theories have been put forward for this condition, there is a treatment which seems to work in cases where there is an overall fungal condition in the animal.

Treatment: A prescribed drug is used to systemically treat guinea pigs with fungal problems so you must see your vet urgently.

Lumps and bumps

Apart from cysts and abscesses, guinea pigs are very prone to many non-malignant lumps and bumps under the surface of the skin. They are seldom attached to bone or tissue and are quite harmless. The most common is one that resembles a jelly bean in size and texture; it is usually found on the tummy. Subcutaneous nodules can often be found running down from the front legs. Any lump that is firmly attached must be investigated promptly and you should consult your vet.

Swimming therapy for paralysis

One of the most common injuries caused by dropping a guinea pig results in paralysis of the hindquarters. Fortunately, there are more cases that result in nerve damage in the vertebrae rather than a break. The acid test is whether there is any sign of residual movement in the feet or back legs. If there is a break, there will be no movement. The animal must be examined properly by a vet and possibly X-rayed.

Together with many other owners, I have used a swimming therapy technique to get a few of these injured animals back on their feet and completely healed. It can also help many more guinea pigs with sufficient mobility in the hindquarters to give them a good quality of life which will run its normal span.

1 Wait for a few days after the fall before beginning therapy and then fill a large, deep bowl with warm water.

2 With one hand supporting the patient underneath and the other steadying it from on top, lower it into the water at an angle to ensure that its head will stay above the surface.

3 Repeat three or four times during the first session and then gradually increase the number of times the animal is lowered into the water in subsequent sessions.

4 Give the guinea pig a good towel rub but don't dry it, for this is part of the therapy. Just watch the way a guinea pig vigorously grooms itself afterwards. This action is as vital as the swimming as it exercises many muscles in the animal's back and strengthens them in the process.

CHAPTER
EIGHT

▌Digestive system

Bloat

This is a very serious condition caused by the build-up of gases or fluid in the gut, usually through a blockage. It is more common in herbivores than carnivores. The symptoms are a distended stomach and refusing all food and liquids.

Treatment: This condition is very hard to treat but there is a measure of success if a gut-relaxing drug is given, followed by 1.5 ml liquid paraffin and frequent massaging of the animal's sides and stomach. I have also had some success using a vibration pad, the kind used by people suffering from arthritic conditions. Expert help is essential for bloat and you must see your vet immediately.

Diarrhoea

This must always be taken very seriously in a guinea pig. As in humans, diarrhoea can be either a very minor problem or a major one. If the guinea pig has running diarrhoea and looks very miserable with its coat puffed up, then it will be in urgent need of some prescribed drug treatment from a vet.

Treatment: You can use an over-the-counter medicine, especially a gut-relaxing drug, if the diarrhoea is very loose. Always rehydrate a guinea pig that is suffering from diarrhoea. If you are inexperienced in such matters or in any doubt, it is best to consult your vet. However, most diarrhoea is just a minor tummy upset.

Administering medicines

■ Administering liquids

Never put medicines in drip feed water bottles. Drugs are effective in measured amounts and there is absolutely no way that an animal can get the correct amount via a water bottle.

■ Administering tablets

Small tablets can be put into the mouth by the method shown.

1 Hold the jaws open with the right hand, then slip the tablet in onto the back teeth with the left hand.

2 Have a small portion of cucumber ready to slip into the mouth as a 'sweetener' to help the animal swallow the tablet.

Note: Larger tablets and pills have to be crushed, mixed with water, then given via a syringe. Always put the syringe in at an angle and push the plunger slowly and gently. It is well worth investing in a pestle and mortar to do the grinding work. Liquid medicine is, of course, administered by syringe. Powdered medicine is best administered upon the back of a teaspoon. Go in at an angle, then wipe the medicine off by scraping the spoon against the top teeth.

Above: *Hold the head firmly and open the jaws with your finger and thumb to administer the medicine.*

Below: *Always use a sweetener, such as a piece of cucumber, to help the medicine go down after you have administered it to your pet.*

CHAPTER
EIGHT

▌Parasites

If your pet is infected by parasites, it is important to treat it quickly before the infestation spreads.

Treatment: Conventional treatment for parasites is by shampooing the affected animal with a head lice shampoo formulated for humans. Shampoo all over, leave on for five minutes and then rinse off. Repeat again in one week's time. One session will only kill the living parasite, not the eggs which have to be killed as soon as they begin to hatch about a week later.

Alternative treatment: This is by the use of Neem oil, using one part Neem oil to three parts carrier oil. Massage into the skin all over, leave on for twenty-four hours and then shampoo off with a good scalp-cleansing shampoo. Repeat after seven days.

Blow fly strike

This happens only in late summer, usually to elderly or infirm guinea pigs. It is caused by a blow fly laying its eggs, usually in the anus of slightly incontinent animals, but sometimes in another orifice or in the skin. The rate at which the larvae grow and multiply is phenomenal. Within twenty to forty-eight hours the animal can be crawling with larvae.

Treatment: The affected guinea pig must be treated immediately by a vet with an appropriate drug.

Prevention: This is always better than cure and if there are any elderly animals in your stock, particularly if they are kept outdoors in late summer, you should dab their rear ends generously with lemon grass, lavender or citronella essential oils. These will act as a non-toxic fly repellent.

Worming

Guinea pigs seldom suffer from intestinal worms but by feeding off the ground they can ingest small parasites that unbalance the gut flora. This is why it is wise to worm them once every three months with a specially formulated product.

Claws

Keep these trimmed. If they get too long, the claws can curl and get caught in hay or crevices as they scurry about. Long claws can also cause strains and even breaks in the small bones of the feet.

Right: *Note the delicacy of the digits of the paws. This is why it is important to keep the claws trimmed. Failure to do so could cause injury if claws get caught when a guinea pig is alarmed. It is the bone that breaks, not the claw.*

▌Urinary infections

CHAPTER
EIGHT

Cystitis

This is caused by an infection of the urinary tract and/or bladder.

■ Symptoms

These commonly include the following:

▓ A squeaking as urine is passed

▓ A stale odour from the genital area

▓ Genital sores and scabs if the condition goes untreated

Cystitis can occur in boars as well as sows and the treatment is the same for both.

Treatment: As in humans, cranberry juice is highly effective in treating this condition. Guinea pig urine is very alkaline and the cranberry juice makes it a little more acidic and therefore less attractive to the bacteria to which the guinea pig is prone. Barley water is also beneficial for there can be soreness and lesions in the urinary tract and these are coated by the viscosity of the barley water, easing the pain of passing urine and giving the lesions a better chance to heal. If there is not an improvement after a few days of these treatments, you should visit your vet and try some antibiotics to clear up the problem.

Note: Commercial barley water will not do the job; it is not viscous enough. You will have to make up your own by boiling pearl barley in water.

Kidney problems

The symptoms of these problems are varied and the condition must be properly diagnosed before being treated. The guinea

Right: *Loss of appetite can be an indication of a more serious underlying health problem.*

pig may have a poor appetite with increased urine output, and symptoms similar to those of cystitis can appear. Usually it is necessary for blood or urine tests to be made before deciding on an appropriate course of treatment by a vet.

Stones

Bladderstones are less of a problem in a sow than a boar. Most stones in sows travel down the urethra and, if they are small enough, with the help of a water-soluble lubricant, they can be eased out.

■ **Symptoms**
These are as follows:
■ High squeaking sounds as the animal urinates
■ A much louder squeak and a lifting of the rump as it finishes
■ In sows, the stone can be felt at the opening of the urethra

Treatment: If the stones are too large, minor surgery is required to remove them. It is far more of a problem in boars for the stones stay in the bladder and unless they can be broken down with drugs more major surgery is required to remove them.

CHAPTER
EIGHT

Heat exhaustion

Heat exhaustion can be avoided completely if the guinea pigs' accommodation is properly shaded in hot weather.

■ Symptoms
- The guinea pig will be unable to stand
- It will have a high respiration rate
- It will be in need of rapid cooling

Treatment: Get a towel, soak it in cold water and wrap the guinea pig in it, but only for a short time as you do not want to go too far and chill it. In essence, as soon as it begins to stir, then take it out and keep it cool. **Do not, repeat, do not immediately give it water.** As guinea pigs invariably have problems swallowing properly, the water could find its way into the lungs. Wait until it has recovered and is taking notice of things, then carefully give it water via a syringe or a hand-held drip feed bottle. During the next twenty-four hours get as much rehydration fluid as possible into the animal.

Heart problems

These must be treated by prescribed drugs from your vet, and the quicker the treatment the better the prognosis. Many guinea pigs who have heart attacks live on into old age.

■ Symptoms
The symptoms of the most common heart problems are identical to those seen in humans.

- Breathing comes in deep gasps from deep down in the diaphragm
- The heart rate is slow

■ The mouth and lips, if they are pink, are cyanosed — they have a blue tinge to them, indicating a lack of sufficient oxygen in the blood

Treatment: This is usually a course of diuretics. If your animal displays any of the symptoms listed above and you feel that it might have a heart problem, you should seek emergency treatment immediately from your vet.

Monitoring breathing, heart beat and temperature

Although you can hear sounds which enable a more in-depth diagnosis of potential problems with a stethoscope, for listening to the basic rate of an animal's breathing and heart beat, and also any clicking sounds which might indicate fluid or mucus in the lungs, the human ear is perfectly adequate.

Just place your ear against the side of the guinea pig just behind its front legs. Remember that the guinea pig has two lungs so listen to both sides!

You can use a thermometer which takes the temperature via the ear in a second. However, these thermometers are quite expensive and you can also use a small old-fashioned type of thermometer with the following proviso: never take the temperature of a sick guinea pig anally as is the standard veterinary practice. Sit the animal comfortably in your lap and put the end of the thermometer in the groin. Leave it there for about three minutes and read the scale, then add one degree to the reading taken. It takes longer this way but many experienced owners consider the invasive anal method to be a cruel one to use upon a sick animal.

CHAPTER
EIGHT

Paralysis

If you wake up one morning and discover that your guinea pig is paralysed in the hind quarters, but in every other respect seems healthy and happy, a simple cure might be to give it a high dosage of a calcium supplement: 1 ml night and morning on the first day; 0.5 ml night and morning for the following two days. There is usually an improvement within twenty-four to thirty-eight hours and the animal is back to normal within four days. However, it is always wise to take your pet to the vet.

All other forms of paralysis that develop through various kinds of illness or injury must be expertly examined and treated by a vet. Failure to do so could result in permanent paralysis or death so do not delay.

Pregnancy problems

Miscarriages that occur early on in a pregnancy seldom cause any problems. You will notice dark red blood on the genitals and usually some on the sow's nose. She will have reingested what little there was to abort and cleaned herself up. Always get the sow checked out by your vet if is she aborts well on into her term when the young are already formed.

At the first sign of dribbling, listlessness, or heavy discharge from the vagina, the sow must be checked thoroughly, for it could be a problem that needs specialist treatment, an X-ray investigation and expert evaluation. This is another case where speed is of the essence and you should take the sow to be examined by your vet as soon as possible.

Small discharges, usually of a light muddy colour, are quite common when a sow is close to littering down. Provided that there are none of the other symptoms described, there is no need for concern about these discharges.

▌Weaning and feeding problems

Sometimes babies arrive with one or both of their forepaws bent inwards. In most cases this is caused by the baby having lain awkwardly in the womb, although very occasionally they can have a genetic deformity in which case there is no flexibility in the paws when you try and straighten them and they should not be forced. However, in most cases the paws can be straightened by a little pressure being applied. If you keep flexing them regularly, invariably they quickly level up after a few days.

If for any reason the mother dies, the best course of action is to put the babies under another lactating sow. It is very rare that a sow will reject another sow's young when they come to her to feed. Not only will she feed them but she will also nurse them as she would her own.

When mother guinea pigs suckle their young, they lick their genitals very vigorously now and again. This is to stimulate them to defecate and urinate. This action can be accomplished by using a cotton bud dipped in warm water.

If there is no lactating sow, the owner must act as surrogate

Above: *If the baby guinea pigs have weaning or feeding problems, ask your vet for advice.*

mother. Most fortified powdered milk supplements which are formulated for convalescing humans are fine. Never feed via a syringe for the first week — use a teaspoon instead. This is because very young guinea pigs tend to suck very hard at the nipple and mother's milk does not come out as easily as it does from a syringe. There is a danger that some of the milk could get into the baby's lungs if syringes are used early on. Even using a teaspoon, or sometimes from ordinary suckling, this can occur.

■ **Symptoms**

These include the following:

▓ Laboured breathing

▓ A loud clicking in the lungs

Treatment: Prompt action can usually clear the lungs. Lay the guinea pig against your chest, head down. Very soon it will begin to struggle and obviously get stressed but it is this stress that is part of the therapy, helping it to breathe more heavily and cough up the fluid. Do this several times, even if the clicking stops right away, to ensure that the lungs are completely clear.

CHAPTER
EIGHT

FIRST AID

Bite wounds

These usually occur around the guinea pig's snout, ears, head and on the rump. If there has been a battle royal, there can be badly torn flesh which will need suturing by a vet. However, most bite wounds are small puncture wounds and can be treated in the same way as the kind of minor skin wounds and abrasions that children suffer in the rough and tumble of play.

Treatment: Use some hydrogen peroxide or a saline solution (salt dissolved in water). If anyone in the family wears contact lenses, then the saline solution they use for rinsing their lenses is excellent for this purpose. After cleaning the wound, dress with either lavender oil or an antiseptic ointment which is harmless if ingested.

Always monitor these wounds for a few days in case they become infected. The symptoms are swelling and pus in the wound. In this case, the pus should be squeezed out immediately and the wound cleaned and redressed with antiseptics. If the wound still does not heal within a few days then a visit to the vet will be necessary so that a drug treatment can be prescribed.

Poisoning

The only form of poisoning that you can treat yourself without recourse to a vet is organic poisoning. It is more often seen in young animals that are not as wise about what they eat. It is usually caused by eating either evergreen plants or bulb plants. It is vital to act immediately the symptoms appear.

■ **Symptoms**
These include: weakness, muscle tremors and a tendency for the head to keep dropping.

Treatment of organic poisoning: Because it may be difficult to confirm that the poisoning is organic it is always best to take the affected animal to the vet immediately. However, if you know that it is organic, quickly grind up a 100 mg charcoal tablet with a little water and feed to the animal straight away. After 30 minutes, administer 1.5 ml liquid paraffin. Keep your pet in a box in a warm place with plenty of hay and some food and water.

Treatment of chemical poisoning: All other forms of poisoning, such as from chemical sprays or eating something that is chemically contaminated, must be treated urgently by a vet. The symptoms are usually either respiratory ones or acute diarrhoea.

Syringe feeding

Syringe feeding is very important to aid the recovery of ailing guinea pigs. The real art is getting the mixtures right; if you don't do this, there is always the risk of compounding the problem by giving your patient diarrhoea. When feeding a guinea pig via a syringe, go into its mouth at an angle and give a little at a time.

FIRST AID

INDEX